SHARING THE WORK: AN ANALYSIS OF THE ISSUES IN WORKSHARING AND JOBSHARING

Noah M. Meltz, Frank Reid, and Gerald S. Swartz

Sharing the Work:
an analysis of the issues
in worksharing
and jobsharing

UNIVERSITY OF TORONTO PRESS
TORONTO BUFFALO LONDON

46191

© University of Toronto Press 1981
Toronto Buffalo London
Printed in Canada

ISBN 0-8020-2383-5

Canadian Cataloguing in Publication Data

Meltz, Noah M.
 Sharing the work: an analysis of the issues
 in worksharing and jobsharing
 Bibliography: p.
 ISBN 0-8020-2383-5
 1. Part-time employment. 2. Employment (Economic
 theory). I. Reid, Frank, 1947- II. Swartz,
 Gerald S., 1941- III. Title.
 HD5110.M44   331.2   C80-094779-7

Contents

Preface

The objective of this study was to create a theoretical model that could be used to assess the feasibility of worksharing and jobsharing in the Canadian labour market, and to outline possible changes in government policy to facilitate such practices. We feel that policies to encourage worksharing deserve serious consideration as a practical response to the problems of layoffs and unemployment. Policies to encourage jobsharing would provide increased flexibility for employers to respond to changes in the demographic composition of the labour force and in employee preferences.

Although all three authors discussed various aspects of the study, Meltz assumed primary responsibility for the theoretical analysis of labour supply in Chapter 3 and the empirical analysis of part-time employment in Chapter 4, Reid was primarily responsible for the analysis of the effect of employment-sharing on labour costs in Chapter 2, and Reid and Meltz collaborated on the empirical analysis of worksharing provisions in collective agreements in Chapter 4 and the implications for government policy in Chapter 5. Swartz provided the impetus for the study, made useful suggestions on the direction of the research at all stages of the project, and made valuable revisions in the entire manuscript.

We emphasize that the opinions and analysis set forth in this study are ours alone and do not reflect the official or unofficial views of the University of Toronto Centre for Industrial Relations or the Ontario

Ministry of Labour. We wish to thank the Ministry, however, for funding and encouraging the background research that has made our work possible. Two staff members of the Ministry of Labour, John Ford and Isabella McTavish, also helped our research by compiling a detailed bibliography on worksharing and jobsharing.

Our thanks are due as well to several individuals whose assistance in this project was invaluable: Gordon Robertson, who gave us useful comments at an early stage of the project; Jane Rose and Frances Schechter, who typed parts of the manuscript; Deborah Campbell, who helped us to administer the project; and Charles Bogue, who provided substantial editorial comment and assistance.

N.M.M., F.R., G.S.S.
Centre for Industrial Relations
University of Toronto

1
Introduction

Worksharing is an attempt to combat unemployment by reducing the number of hours each employee works rather than laying employees off when there is a reduction in demand for labour. There has been considerable discussion concerning the extent to which factors other than layoffs have contributed to the high unemployment rates which Canada faces as it enters the 1980s, such as high turnover rates and inadequate skills or experience among the unemployed (see Economic Council of Canada 1976; Reid and Meltz 1979). There is general agreement, however, that a substantial part of the unemployment problem is due simply to the lack of sufficient jobs. In economic terms, part of the unemployment problem is due to increased frictional and structural unemployment but part also to deficient-demand unemployment.

Virtually everyone agrees that full employment for everyone who wants to work is a critical economic goal. The problem, however, is that although governments recognize the need to reduce deficient-demand unemployment by adopting expansionary fiscal and monetary policies, they have hesitated to do so because they fear that such policies will fuel inflation (see Reid 1980). Because of their concern with inflation, governments have tolerated and perhaps even contributed to high unemployment levels through fiscal restraint and spending cutbacks. Since deficient-demand unemployment is unlikely to be completely eliminated in the near future we feel that worksharing deserves serious consideration as one policy to reduce the severity of the problem. Jobsharing and regular part-time employment are related to worksharing. The distinction between them is that, whereas worksharing is designed to protect workers' jobs when the demand for labour is deficient, jobsharing and regular part-time employment are intended to accommodate persons who prefer to work less than full-time.[1] Jobsharing differs from part-time employment in that jobsharing allows two or more workers to share a job that was (or could be) filled by one full-time worker, while a regular part-time job is work that for technical or cost reasons cannot easily be converted into a full-time job.[2]

Our interest in jobsharing and regular part-time work has been stimulated by two aspects of the changing demography of the labour force during the 1970s. First, changes in social attitudes have led to an increase in the participation rates of women, especially married women, in the labour force. The resulting increase in the number of multiple-earner families in the labour force can be expected to intensify the desire for employment in jobs that demand less than full-time participation. Second, the post-war baby boom has increased the importance of the 15-to-24-year age group in the population. Individuals in this group may be interested in part-time employment and jobsharing because they want more education and training and because they typically have fewer family responsibilities. Unfortunately, most regular part-time jobs in the past have been predominantly low-skill, low-wage jobs (Owen 1978). Jobsharing has been suggested as a way of making challenging, high-skill jobs accessible to men and women who want to pursue a career but prefer not to work full-time.

Although the impetus for jobsharing and part-time employment is very different from that for worksharing, many of the factors that must be considered in analysing the costs and benefits of these measures are

1 Persons who are working part-time involuntarily (i.e., those who would prefer a full-time job at the same wage rate) are thus involved in 'worksharing' rather than 'regular part-time employment' according to our definitions.
2 For ease of exposition we shall speak of dividing one job between two or more workers, but the definition can be applied more generally to the division of x jobs between y workers where $y > x$. Although one normally thinks of dividing a full-time job, the definition also applies to the division of part-time jobs.

similar – for example, the effects they have on labour costs, the types of workers likely to support them, and the economic situations in which working less than full time is likely to be attractive or acceptable. Because of these similarities we shall introduce a new term, *employment-sharing*, which comprises worksharing, jobsharing, and regular part-time employment.

ORGANIZATION OF THIS STUDY

In Chapter 2 we consider the implications of employment-sharing for labour demand by analysing its effects on labour costs. In Chapter 3 we turn to the question of labour supply, considering the implications of employment-sharing for employees and the types of employees who are most apt to want to engage in it. In Chapter 4 we bring labour supply and demand together to predict the circumstances under which employment-sharing is most likely to occur. By comparing the empirical predictions made in this chapter with the actual incidence of employment-sharing in various industries and demographic groups, we are able to test our analysis of the determinants of employment-sharing. In chapter 5 we use the model to assess the economic merits of employment-sharing and, where warranted, to recommend changes in policy to encourage (or discourage) employment-sharing. In the final chapter we summarize the results of our study and its policy implications.

2
The costs of employment-sharing

WHY COSTS ARE IMPORTANT

This chapter examines the implications of employment-sharing for demand for labour through an analysis of the effects of employment-sharing on the employer's unit labour costs.

It is important to consider the effect of employment-sharing on labour costs for three reasons. First, a firm's willingness to implement any program will depend on the effect it has on costs. Second, an analysis of the effect that employment-sharing programs have on costs will help in assessing their social desirability and in determining what types of industries or firms are best suited to such programs. Third, if the government decides to encourage employment-sharing, an analysis of its costs will help in developing policies to achieve this objective.

In analysing the effect of employment-sharing on labour costs we shall construct our economic model in three stages: a simple model with only fixed and variable costs; a richer model that includes 'quasi-fixed' costs; and an extension of the analysis to consider effects on productivity, the seniority mix of employees, and the nature of product demand. We shall then apply the model to recent Ontario data to make a preliminary empirical assessment of the magnitude of the effect that 'typical' worksharing and jobsharing programs will have on costs.

A THEORETICAL MODEL WITH FIXED AND
VARIABLE COSTS

Economists assume that firms attempt to maximize profits, implying that a firm will employ additional labour only if the extra revenue generated by its employment is greater than or equal to the costs of employing it. The costs involved are to be interpreted broadly as including the hourly wage rate, fringe benefits, training costs, and other costs. For a given state of technology, a firm's output depends on its capital stock (its plant and machinery) and the total hours of labour employed. The law of diminishing returns implies that, when capital stock is fixed, the extra output obtained by employing each additional hour of labour will decline as more hours of labour are employed. A firm will maximize its profits when the amount of labour it employs is such that the value of the extra output produced by the last hour of labour is just equal to the hourly wage rate (see Figure 1).

In this model, which is the one typically encountered in introductory and intermediate economics, the conditions for maximizing profit determine the total number of hours of labour employed, but the firm is indifferent as to how its total hours of labour are distributed between hours per worker and number of workers. In other words, the firm may employ many workers, each working only a few hours, or it may employ few workers, each working many hours; the firm does not care as long as the total number of hours necessary to maximize profits has been obtained.[1] Thus, in this simple model employment-sharing has no effect on a firm's costs.

The reason this is so in the above model is that it includes only two types of costs, variable and fixed. Variable costs are those that are affected by the level of output, such as wages and raw materials. Fixed costs are all costs that are not affected by the level of output, such as overhead costs on the plant. Since output is dependent on the total number of labour hours employed (L), we can also say that variable costs are those that are related to L and fixed costs are those not related to L.

---

1 By definition $L \equiv EH$, where L in the total hours of labour, H is the hours per employee, and E is the total number of employees.

8 Sharing the work

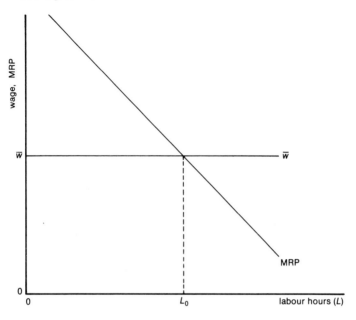

Figure 1   The determination of total hours of labour employed

In this figure $\bar{w}$ represents the wage rate determined in the labour market or by collective agreement. The marginal revenue product (MRP) curve shows the extra revenue to the firm generated by employing each additional hour of labour. Profits are maximized at L_0, where MRP equals the wage rate.

A THEORETICAL MODEL WITH QUASI-FIXED COSTS

Critical in assessing the effect of employment-sharing on unit labour costs is that category of costs wholly or partially related to the number of employees rather than to the total number of labour hours. These costs will be called 'quasi-fixed' after Oi (1962), who discusses labour as a quasi-fixed factor of production.[2]

2 In symbols we can express total costs (TC) per week for the firm as $TC = TFC + TVC + TQC$, where TFC is total fixed costs, TVC is total variable costs, and TQC is total quasi-fixed costs. By definition, total variable costs are related to L and total quasi-fixed costs are related to E: $TVC = g(L)$, $TQC = h(E)$.

Some examples of cost categories that include a quasi-fixed cost are hiring and training costs and many fringe benefits such as employer contributions to Unemployment Insurance, the Canada Pension Plan, Workmen's Compensation, and health insurance plans. The extent to which these costs are quasi-fixed costs depends on the particulars of the plans and will be discussed in detail below.

As an example of a pure quasi-fixed cost, consider a firm that pays a fixed amount in health insurance premiums for each employee. If on the one hand output were expanded by increasing the number of employees, the firm's medical premiums would increase, and they would resemble variable costs. If on the other hand output were expanded by increasing the hours each employee works, there would be no increase in health insurance premiums, and they would resemble a fixed cost. This fact explains the sense in which health insurance premiums are a 'quasi-fixed' cost. As Figure 2a shows, a fringe benefit is a pure quasi-fixed cost if the fringe benefit cost per employee is unrelated to earnings per employee.[3]

Not all fringe benefits are quasi-fixed costs. For example, if vacation pay is specified as 4 per cent of annual earnings, the fringe cost per employee is proportional to earnings per employee (Figure 2b), and the fringe is a pure variable cost. In such a case the total cost of the fringe is a function of the total number of labour hours, and its effect is the same as that of a 4 per cent increase in the wage rate.[4]

Some fringe benefits combine features of both quasi-fixed costs and variable costs. For some types of benefits (e.g. Unemployment Insurance) there is a ceiling $(\overline{wH})$ on employee earnings subject to contribution. For such cases (Figure 2c), the fringe is a variable cost for employees earning below the ceiling and a quasi-fixed cost for employees

---

3 For a pure quasi-fixed cost the average cost per employee for a fringe benefit (f) is expressed by $f = a$, where a is a constant. The fringe benefit cost for all employees (F) is then $F = fE = aE$, i.e. proportional to the number of employees.

4 Average fringe cost per employee is $f = b(wH)$, where b is a constant and w is average hourly earnings. Total cost of the fringe is $F = bwHE$, and substituting it in the definition $L \equiv EH$ implies that $F = bwL$, i.e. F is proportional to total labour hours L.

earning above the ceiling. Figure 2d illustrates a case (e.g. the Canada Pension Plan) in which the fringe benefit applies only to earnings above the minimum exemption level $(wH)^*$. For employees earning below $(wH)^*$ the fringe cost is zero and hence is not a cost at all. For employees earning above $(wH)^*$, and for a given number of total labour hours of employment, costs will be reduced by an increase in the number of employees.[5] This point will be developed further in the simulations analysis below.

A firm's reaction to employment sharing will of course be affected by a much broader range of considerations than the effect on quasi-fixed costs. We turn now to an examination of some of these other effects.

THE EFFECTS OF EMPLOYMENT-SHARING ON
PRODUCTIVITY

Increasing the number of hours each employee works has the advantage of reducing quasi-fixed costs. To maximize its profits, however, a firm must balance these advantages against several disadvantages.

One disadvantage of increasing the number of hours each employee works is that beyond a specified level overtime wages must be paid. Another disadvantage is that if employees are required to work too many hours they will become fatigued and their productivity will drop.[6] More generally, as the analysis of labour supply in the next chapter indicates, given the wage rates and the employees' tastes for income and leisure time, there is an optimal number of hours of labour that employees will wish to supply each week. If a firm demands a

5 For a fringe benefit with a ceiling, the fringe function becomes
$$f = \begin{cases} b(wH) & \text{for } wH < \overline{wH}, \\ b(\overline{wH}) & \text{for } wH \geq \overline{wH}, \end{cases}$$
where $(\overline{wH})$ is the maximum earnings per employee on which fringe benefits are payable. For a fringe with an exemption level the fringe function becomes
$$f = \begin{cases} 0 & \text{for } wH < (wH)^*, \\ b[wH-(wH)^*] & \text{for } wH \geq (wH)^*. \end{cases}$$
6 Formally, hours per employee (H) and total labour hours (L) both enter the production function; employee fatigue implies diminishing marginal returns to H as well as to L.

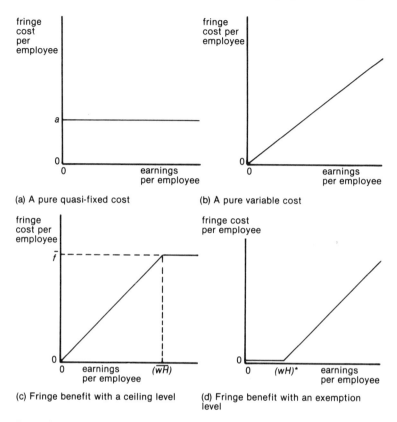

Figure 2   Illustration of fringe benefit costs

work week of greater or fewer than the optimal number of hours, then, other things equal, the firm will experience more difficulty attracting workers. These supply considerations must be balanced against demand (cost) considerations in reaching the final equilibrium for both the worker and the firm.

These factors are significant in determining the feasibility of employment-sharing. If the average hourly product declines as the number of hours worked by each employee increases, any increase in quasi-fixed costs that results from the introduction of employment-sharing will be partially offset by an increase in the average productivity. It has also been suggested that employment-sharing will increase productivity by reducing absenteeism since employees will have more time to conduct personal business, recover from illnesses, or engage in leisure activities. To the extent that absenteeism is related to these factors, employment-sharing will reduce absenteeism and thus increase productivity. However, productivity may actually be reduced by the 'Monday-morning' low-productivity syndrome. If there is a weekly 'start-up' time characterized by low productivity, then employment-sharing may lower the average productivity still further by increasing the proportion of total work time in these low-productivity periods.

The effect of employment-sharing on a firm's costs is influenced as well by the fact that employees are a heterogeneous group with different skills, levels of productivity, and earnings. For example, when a firm lays workers off the remaining workers are sometimes 'bumped' into new jobs, a process that can increase costs if the firm's work force is heterogeneous. Work-sharing circumvents this problem by distributing the reductions in hours equally among junior and senior employees. If the firm uses a system of laying off its least senior workers, layoffs will generally increase the average wage, since the more senior employees will earn higher wages. One may argue that the increase in the average wage will not increase the average costs if the productivity of the senior workers is higher than that of the junior workers by the same proportion as their wage rates, but it remains true that junior workers are usually more physically vigorous and perhaps better educated than senior workers. Whether senior employees are able to compensate in experience for what they lack in education and physical vigour is an empirical question that cannot be answered here. In any case, worksharing avoids an increase in the average wage because all employees are equally affected by the reduction in hours.

A firm's attitude toward the use of part-time employees can also be affected by the nature of the demand for its product. For example, many service industries face peak periods of the week (or day) characterized by high demand, interspersed with slack periods. In these situations it may be better to employ regular part-time workers than to employ full-time workers, because part-time workers can be scheduled to meet the peak periods of demand without resorting to split shifts. Employment-sharing can thus reduce labour costs and at the same time allow firms to use work schedules better suited to employee preferences.

AN EMPIRICAL ANALYSIS OF THE COST IMPLICATIONS OF WORKSHARING

Table 1 contains data on the average amounts that employers contribute to various fringe benefit plans annually for each employee. This table shows that in 1976 firms in Canada spent an average of over $1000 a year for each employee on contributions to various benefit plans, in this way adding 9 per cent to annual earnings. These costs are quite large. Clearly it is important to examine the effect that employment-sharing will have on them.

In this and the following section we shall use the theoretical model developed above to make a rough assessment of the empirical magnitude of the effect that employment-sharing has on labour costs. First we consider the effect of a representative worksharing scheme implemented in response to a 20 per cent reduction in labour hours (for example, a reduction from a five-day to a four-day work week). Then we shall examine the effect on costs of a representative jobsharing or part-time employment program in which one full-time job is replaced by two half-time jobs. The figures used in these simulations are based on costs in Ontario during 1978.

Unemployment Insurance contributions
In 1978 employees contributed 1.5 per cent of their annual earnings up to a maximum annual wage of $12,480 in unemployment insurance (UI) premiums. Company contributions were 1.4 times the employee contribution, i.e. 1.4(1.5%) = 2.1 per cent of annual earnings.[7]

Table 2 shows a hypothetical firm's UI contribution costs in two alternative situations, a layoff (in which four employees are employed full-time and one employee is laid off) and a worksharing scheme (in which all five employees remain and work 80 per cent of a normal work

---

7 Thus, for UI contributions the fringe formula becomes
$$f = \begin{cases} 0.021(wH) & \text{for } wH < \$12{,}480, \\ 0.021(12{,}480) & \text{for } wH \geq \$12{,}480. \end{cases}$$

TABLE 1
Company contributions to employee benefit plans, all-industry average,
Canada, 1976

Item	Annual expenditure per employee in dollars	Percentage of annual earnings
Workmen's Compensation	211	1.8
Unemployment Insurance	168	1.4
Canada or Quebec Pension Plan	129	1.1
Private pension plans	357	3.0
Life and health insurance plans	186	1.6
Other	24	0.2
Total contributions	1,075	9.0
Annual earnings	11,973	100.0
Total compensation	13,948	109.0

SOURCE: Statistics Canada, *Labour Costs in Canada—All Industry*

week). Figure 3 shows graphically the absolute and percentage differences in costs between these two situations, plotted against employee earnings. Company UI contributions cause labour costs in the worksharing scheme to exceed those in the layoff when full-time employee earnings are above the ceiling level of $12,480 a year. The effect varies from a minimum of zero to a maximum of just under one-half of one per cent.

There is an intuitive explanation of why the effect of worksharing on labour costs varies with the earnings of the employees involved. If employees are earning less than the ceiling of $12,480 a year, employer UI contributions are proportional to earnings; UI contributions are then a pure variable cost rather than a quasi-fixed cost, and worksharing has no effect on company UI contributions. If the full-time employees are earning over $12,480, however, worksharing does affect labour costs. Since the firm's total payroll is the same in both the worksharing and layoff cases, it is to the firm's advantage to have as high a fraction as possible of its payroll eligible for exemption, i.e. accruing to workers earnings over $12,400 a year. Worksharing reduces the earnings of those workers who would have made between $12,480 and $15,600 full-time to below the $12,480 ceiling and thus eliminates the fraction of the

TABLE 2

The effect of worksharing on the cost of company contributions to Unemployment Insurance ($)

	Layoff situation: four full-time employees and one employee on layoff			Worksharing situation: five employees working 80% of full-time			Cost difference between layoff situation and worksharing situation	
(1) Earnings per full-time employee	(2) UI contributions per full-time employee	(3) Total UI contributions		(4) Earnings per worksharing employee	(5) UI Contributions per worksharing employee	(6) Total UI contributions	(7) Absolute difference	(8) Difference as percentage of total earnings
1,000	21.00	84.00		800	16.80	84.00	0	0
5,000	105.00	420.00		4,000	84.00	420.00	0	0
10,000	210.00	840.00		8,000	168.00	840.00	0	0
15,000	262.08	1048.32		12,000	252.00	1260.00	211.68	0.35
20,000	262.08	1048.32		16,000	262.08	1310.40	262.08	0.33
25,000	262.08	1048.32		20,000	262.08	1310.40	262.08	0.26
30,000	262.08	1048.32		24,000	262.08	1310.40	262.08	0.22

NOTE: Column (1) shows the income of those workers who remain employed when layoffs take place. Column (2) shows the employer's UI contribution for each employee. Column (3) shows the total UI contributions for the four employees (column (3) = 4 X column (2)). Columns (4), (5), and (6) give the corresponding information for the worksharing scheme under which five employees each work 80 per cent of a full work week. Column (7) shows the absolute difference between the employer contributions required in the worksharing and layoff situations. Column (8) gives this difference as a percentage of total employee income (i.e. for four full-time employees or five worksharing employees).

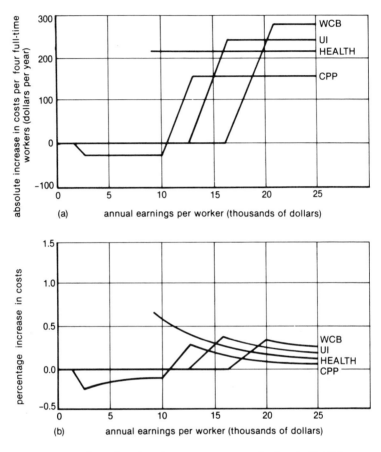

Figure 3   The effect of worksharing on company contributions to UI, CPP, Workmen's Compensation, and health insurance

payroll that would have been exempt from company UI contributions. Thus, in this wage range worksharing increases the firm's UI contribution costs, and the amount of the cost increase rises as employee earnings rise.

The absolute increase in costs is greatest when full-time employee earnings reach $15,600 a year. The reason is that at this income level employment-sharing does not reduce the income of any workers below the $12,480 ceiling. The employer must pay full UI contributions for five employees under worksharing instead of four under layoffs. The extra cost of worksharing is the maximum contribution for one worker, i.e. $262 a year. This cost is constant in absolute dollars for incomes over $15,600, but it declines as a percentage of total labour costs as annual employee income increases.

Canada Pension Plan
In 1978 company contributions to the Canada Pension Plan (CPP) were 1.8 per cent of all employee earnings above the minimum exemption of $1000 a year and below the maximum of $10,400 a year.[8] Table 3 shows the firm's CPP contribution costs in both the layoff and worksharing situations, again considering the case of a 20 per cent reduction in total hours of employment.

Since there is both an exemption and a maximum on earnings subject to contribution, the pattern for the CPP costs is more complex than that for the UI costs. If employees earn less than $1000 a year (without layoffs or worksharing) then the firm makes no CPP contributions at all in either the worksharing or the layoff case, and there is obviously no effect on contribution costs. If employees earn between $1000 and $10,400 a year, worksharing can actually *reduce* the company's CPP contribution costs. The reason is that the gross payroll is the same in a layoff and in worksharing, but in the latter the basic $1000 minimum exemption applies to five employees instead of only four employees as in a layoff. This extra $1000 of exempted payroll saves the firm 0.018 ($1000) = $18 a year. If employees earn over $10,400 a year full-time, worksharing tends to increase costs because it reduces the portion of the firm's total payroll that accrues to workers earning over $10,400 a year and thus reduces the amount of the payroll exempt from CPP contributions. For employees earning over $10,650 full-time, this effect exceeds the reduction in costs due to the $1000 exemption, and the net effect of worksharing is to increase costs. The absolute increase in costs is greatest for employees whose full-time earnings are $13,000 a year.

8 The fringe function for the CPP contribution may be expressed as

$$f = \begin{array}{ll} 0 & \text{for } wH \geq \$1000 \\ 0.018(wH - 1000) & \text{for } \$1000 < wH < \$10,400, \\ 0.018(10,400 - 1000) & \text{for } wH \geq \$10,400. \end{array}$$

TABLE 3

The effect of worksharing on the cost of company contributions to the Canada Pension Plan ($)

Layoff situation: four full-time employees and one employee on layoff			Worksharing situation: five employees working 80% of full-time			Cost difference between layoff situation and worksharing situation	
(1) Earnings per full-time employee	(2) CPP contributions per full-time employee	(3) Total CPP contributions	(4) Earnings per worksharing employee	(5) CPP contributions per worksharing employee	(6) Total CPP contributions	(7) Absolute difference	(8) Difference as percentage of total earnings
1,000	0	0	800	0	0	0	0
5,000	72.00	288.00	4,000	54.00	270	−18.00	−0.09
10,000	162.00	648.00	8,000	126.00	630	−18.00	−0.05
15,000	169.20	676.80	12,000	169.20	846	169.20	0.28
20,000	169.20	676.80	16,000	169.20	846	169.20	0.21
25,000	169.20	676.80	20,000	169.20	846	169.20	0.17
30,000	169.20	676.80	24,000	169.20	846	169.20	0.14

NOTE: Column (1) shows the income of those workers who remain employed when layoffs take place. Column (2) shows the employer's CPP contribution for each employee. Column (3) shows the total CPP contribution for the four employees (column (3) = 4 X column (2)). Columns (4), (5), and (6) give the corresponding information for the worksharing scheme under which five employees each work 80 per cent of a full work week. Column (7) shows the absolute difference between the employer contributions required in the worksharing and layoff situations. Column (8) gives this difference as a percentage of total employee income (i.e. for four full-time employees or five worksharing employees).

The increase is $169.20 a year, the extra CPP maximum contribution for one full-time employee (five employees in worksharing situation but only four in the layoff situation), and it corresponds to an increase in labour costs of 0.33 per cent at the $13,000 wage level (Figure 3 shows graphically the absolute and percentage increases in costs due to CPP contributions).

Workmen's Compensation
Company contributions to the Ontario Workmen's Compensation Board (WCB) in 1978 were a percentage of employee earnings up to a ceiling of $16,200, the percentage varying with the accident record of the industry. Table 1 showed that the average contribution rate was 1.8 per cent in Canada in 1976.[9]

Table 4 shows the company's WCB contribution costs in the hypothetical layoff and worksharing situations that we have used throughout this section. When the employees' full-time earnings are less than the $16,200 ceiling, worksharing has no effect on company costs. When the employees' full-time earnings exceed $16,200, worksharing increases costs by reducing the proportion of the total wage bill that is exempt from employer contributions because it accrues to workers earning over the ceiling. The absolute difference reaches a maximum of $291.60 when the level of full-time earnings is $16,200/0.8 = $20,250 a year. At this level the absolute difference due to worksharing corresponds to an increase in labour costs of 0.36 per cent of the total wage bill (Figure 3 shows the absolute and percentage cost differences due to work-sharing).

PRIVATE PENSIONS, LIFE INSURANCE, AND
HEALTH INSURANCE

Table 1 showed that company contributions to private pension plans were an average of 3.0 per cent of annual earnings in 1976 and that contributions to life and medical insurance plans added another 1.6 per

9 The fringe function for WCB contribution costs may be expressed as
$$f = \begin{cases} 0.018wH & \text{for } wH < \$16{,}200, \\ 0.018(16{,}200) & \text{for } wH \geqslant \$16{,}200. \end{cases}$$

TABLE 4

The effect of worksharing on the cost of company contributions to Workmen's Compensation ($)

(1) Earnings per full-time employee	Layoff situation: four full-time employees and one employee on layoff		Worksharing situation: five employees working 80% of full-time			Cost difference between layoff situation and worksharing situation	
	(2) WCB contributions per full-time employee	(3) Total WCB contributions	(4) Earnings per worksharing employee	(5) WCB contributions per worksharing employee	(6) Total WCB contributions	(7) Absolute difference	(8) Difference as percentage of total earnings
1,000	18.00	72.00	800	14.40	72.00	0	0
5,000	90.00	360.00	4,000	72.00	360.00	0	0
10,000	180.00	720.00	8,000	144.00	720.00	0	0
15,000	270.00	1,080.00	12,000	216.00	1,080.00	0	0
20,000	291.60	1,166.40	16,000	288.00	1,440.00	273.60	0.34
25,000	291.60	1,166.40	20,000	291.60	1,458.00	291.60	0.29
30,000	291.60	1,166.40	24,000	291.60	1,458.00	291.60	0.24

NOTE: Column (1) shows the income of those workers who remain employed when layoffs take place. Column (2) shows the employer's WCB contribution for each employee. Column (3) shows the total WCB contribution for the four employees (column (3) = 4 X column (2)). Columns (4), (5), and (6) give the corresponding information for the worksharing scheme under which five employees each work 80 per cent of a full work week. Column (7) shows the absolute difference between the employer contributions required in the worksharing and layoff situations. Column (8) gives this difference as a percentage of total employee income (i.e. for four full-time employees or five worksharing employees).

cent. In the absence of detailed information on the plans at various companies we shall make a rough estimate of the effect that work-sharing would have on company contribution costs by assuming that contributions to pension plans are proportional to earnings and contributions to life and health insurance plans are independent of earnings. Since pension contributions are assumed to be proportional to earnings, they are a pure variable cost; worksharing will have no effect on them. Since health-plan costs are independent of earnings, they are a quasi-fixed cost and will be higher under any worksharing agreement than if a layoff were imposed. In 1976 company contributions to life and health insurance plans were an average of $186 per employee each year. Inflated by the rise in the Consumer Price Index (CPI), this contribution comes to $222 for each employee in 1978. Thus, under a worksharing agreement in which five employees share the work of four full-time employees a company must contribute $222 more a year in health and life insurance premiums than if it had retained only four full-time employees and laid off one employee. As a percentage of the gross payroll this added cost declines as employee earnings rise; when full-time employee earnings are $15,000 a year it constitutes an increase of 0.37 per cent.

Figure 3 shows the absolute and proportional differences that worksharing makes in contribution costs. Because it is unlikely that the health insurance premiums of employees with relatively low annual earnings will be paid by their employers, we have assumed, in the absence of easily accessible data, that employers did not pay health insurance premiums for workers earning $5,000 a year or less.

Hiring and training costs
One of the advantages of worksharing from the firm's viewpoint is that under a worksharing arrangement it is more likely to retain the work force that it will need when demand increases and the firm expands its output. If the firm lays employees off it is more likely that these employees will obtain work with other firms or leave in search of employment elsewhere, or that their skills will deteriorate during the layoff.[10]

10 In algebraic terms, let n be the number of employees, p be the proportion laid off, r be the proportion of laid-off workers who will need to be replaced

It is very difficult to estimate the size of a firm's cost savings due to worksharing because it is almost impossible to foresee what proportion of laid-off workers would leave the firm during a layoff. The proportion of workers lost would be affected by such factors as the expected and actual duration of the layoff, opportunities for employment and earnings elsewhere, and the amount of seniority the workers had accumulated.

Data on the costs of hiring and training replacements for those employees who leave are also difficult to obtain. However, a recent study by the Ontario Ministry of Labour reports that in 1975 'replacement costs range from $3,000 to $7,000 for the average employee according to the method of hiring. These figures include direct and indirect costs such as those incurred in advertising the position, holding interviews, training and orienting the new employee, and lower productivity due to inexperience' (Robertson and Humphreys 1978, 42).

As an illustration of the potential effect of these replacement costs consider a firm in which replacement costs are $5000 for each worker, 20 per cent of the work force is laid off for a three-month period, 5 per cent of the laid-off workers must be replaced, and full-time workers earn $15,000 a year. If these estimates are used the cost of replacing lost workers is 1.7 per cent of the gross payroll during the layoff period.[11] If these figures represent the approximate order of magnitude of replacement costs they suggest that the cost advantage of worksharing over layoffs as a response to a temporary reduction in the demand for labour is substantial.

when demand expands, and c be cost in dollars per worker of replacement. The total cost of replacing workers lost because of the layoff then equals $crpn$. If the annual level of earnings is Y dollars and the fraction of the year that the layoff lasts is t, then the gross payroll during the layoff is $t(1 - p)$ Yn. Worker replacement costs as a fraction of the gross payroll for the period of the layoff (x) are then

$x = crp/t(1 - p)Y$.

11 Substitution into the expression in the previous footnote gives

$$x = \frac{(5,000)(0.20)(0.05)}{(0.25)(0.80)(15,000)} = 0.017 = 1.7\%,$$

where $c = 5,000, p = 0.20, t = 0.25, r = 0.05$, and $Y = 15,000$.

TABLE 5
Increase in costs for a firm adopting worksharing rather than layoffs ($)

(1)	Absolute increase in costs					Increase in costs as a percentage of gross payroll				
Annual earnings	(2) Unemployment Insurance	(3) Canada Pension Plan	(4) Workmen's Compensation	(5) Health premiums	(6) Sum of all four fringes	(7) Unemployment Insurance	(8) Canada Pension Plan	(9) Workmen's Compensation	(10) Health premiums	(11) Sum of all four fringes
1,000	0	0	0	0	0	0	0	0	0	0
5,000	0	−18.00	0	0	−18.0	0	−0.09	0	0	−0.09
10,000	0	−18.00	0	222.00	203.99	0	−0.04	0	0.55	0.50
15,000	211.67	169.20	0	222.00	602.87	0.35	0.28	0	0.37	1.00
20,000	262.08	169.20	273.59	222.00	926.87	0.32	0.21	0.34	0.27	1.15
25,000	262.08	169.20	291.60	222.00	944.87	0.29	0.16	0.29	0.22	0.94
30,000	262.08	169.20	291.60	222.00	944.87	0.24	0.14	0.24	0.18	0.78

NOTE: Column (1) shows the given level of full-time income. Columns (2), (3), (4), and (5) show the absolute increase in costs for UI premiums, CPP, Workmen's Compensation, and health insurance, respectively, when worksharing is adopted instead of a layoff. Column (6) is the sum of columns (2), (3), (4), and (5), and shows the absolute cost increase of all four fringe benefits combined. Columns (7), (8), (9), and (10) show the proportional increase in costs from each of the four fringe benefit programs. Column (11) shows the total increase in costs from the four programs as a percentage of the total earnings of four full-time employees.

The net effect of worksharing on labour costs
Table 5 summarizes the net increase in costs due to contributions to Unemployment Insurance, the Canada Pension Plan, Workmen's Compensation, private pension plans, and health insurance plans. The same information is shown in Figure 4.

This simulation yields some important results. First, the use of worksharing rather than layoffs increases the cost to the firm of the four benefits examined above. Second, the magnitude of the increase in costs is about 0.5 per cent to 1.0 per cent of the gross payroll; though an increase of this size can deter employers from engaging in worksharing, it has probably been exaggerated in some discussions of the issue. Third, worksharing increases the firm's UI, WCB, and CPP costs only because there are ceilings on the annual earnings subject to contribution in each case. The ceiling levels on earnings subject to contribution varied from $10,400 a year to $16,200 a year in 1978. Given these figures, worksharing has little effect on costs for employees who earn less than $10,000 a year, but it increases costs steadily for those who earn up to about $21,000 a year. At this point the cost increase in absolute dollars ceases, and cost increases as a proportion of total payroll decline as the annual earnings of each employee rise above $21,000.

Another important conclusion of the analysis is that worksharing can *reduce costs* for the firm because fewer employees will leave the firm for work elsewhere during the layoff period. The estimates of cost savings made in this study were very crude because of the lack of reliable data on the fraction of workers a firm would have to replace after a layoff and on the costs of hiring and training a replacement. However, assuming that the firm would have to replace only 5 per cent of the workers it laid off, and using the best available data on replacement costs, we estimate that a firm which engaged in worksharing rather than layoffs would save about 1.7 per cent of its payroll. If this estimate is reasonable, the savings from reduced replacement costs would *more than offset* the increase in the costs of employer contributions to fringe benefits, which we estimated to be about 0.5 to 1.0 per cent of the total payroll. This is clearly a matter of crucial importance, and further research is needed to establish the savings more precisely.

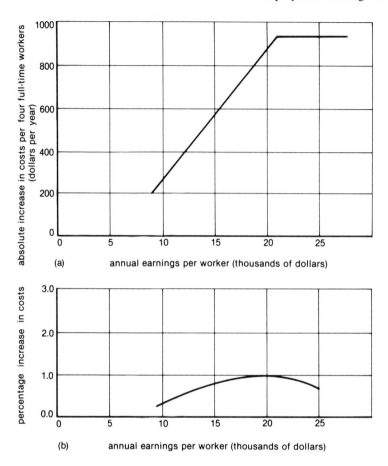

Figure 4   The effect of worksharing on contribution costs: sum of UI, CPP, Workmen's Compensation, and health insurance

An empirical analysis of the cost implications
of jobsharing and part-time work
In this section we examine the effect on costs of a representative job-sharing scheme in which one full-time employee is replaced by two

half-time employees. The analysis also indicates the increase in costs that would occur if one full-time employee were replaced by two part-time employees working half the normal hours and receiving the same fringe benefits.

The simulations assume that fringe benefits are prorated as far as possible. It is assumed, for example, that the firm pays one-half of the cost of health premiums for each of the jobsharing employees, so that there is no increase in this regard. For the three statutory programs, however, prorating is not possible, and the effect on labour costs is analysed.

Since the analysis is similar to that in the previous section, the various fringe benefits are not analysed in detail. A summary of the results is presented in Table 6, and the absolute and percentage increases in costs are shown in Figures 5 and 6.

Table 6 shows that the results are similar to those for worksharing. Costs are barely affected when an employee's earnings are below the ceiling levels for contributions. The absolute increase in costs is greatest when employees earn above $30,000 a year, but the increase in costs as a percentage of gross payroll is much more substantial than in the case of worksharing because the cost increase is a percentage of the earnings of only one full-time worker rather than four. The cost increase is roughly 2 per cent, twice as high as in the representative worksharing example.

An important difference between worksharing and jobsharing concerns replacement costs. A major advantage of worksharing was the possibility of substantial savings through a reduction in the number of workers who would need to be replaced. With jobsharing, however, such is not the case. If turnover remained unchanged the representative jobsharing program being analysed would result in a doubling of replacement costs. Very likely jobsharing would result in some reduction of the turnover rate, but unless the latter were cut in half there would still be some increase in replacement costs.

Another potential disadvantage of jobsharing is increased supervisory or administrative costs, although the increase in supervisory costs could be minimized by sufficient communication between the jobsharing employees.

TABLE 6
Increase in costs for a firm adopting jobsharing ($)

(1)	Absolute increase in costs					Increase in costs as a percentage of gross payroll				
	(2)	(3)	(4)	(5)	(6)	(7)	(8)	(9)	(10)	(11)
Annual earnings	Unemployment Insurance	Canada Pension Plan	Workmen's Compensation	Health premiums	Sum of all four fringes	Unemployment Insurance	Canada Pension Plan	Workmen's Compensation	Health premiums	Sum of all four fringes
1,000	0	0	0	0	0	0	0	0	0	0
5,000	0	−18.00	0	0	−18.00	0	−0.36	0	0	−0.36
10,000	0	−18.00	0	0	−18.00	0	−0.18	0	0	−0.18
15,000	52.91	64.79	0	0	117.71	0.35	0.43	0	0	0.78
20,000	157.92	154.79	68.39	0	381.11	0.78	0.77	0.34	0	1.91
25,000	262.08	169.20	158.39	0	589.67	1.04	0.67	0.63	0	2.36
30,000	262.08	169.20	248.39	0	679.67	0.87	0.56	0.82	0	2.27

NOTE: Column (1) shows the given level of full-time income. Columns (2), (3), (4), and (5) show the absolute increase in costs for UI premiums, CPP, Workmen's Compensation, and health insurance, respectively, when jobsharing is adopted. Column (6) is the sum of columns (2), (3), (4), and (5), and shows the absolute cost increase of all four fringe benefits combined. Columns (7), (8), (9), and (10) show the proportional increase in costs from each of the four fringe benefit programs. Column (11) shows the total increase in costs from the four programs as a percentage of the total earnings of one full-time employee.

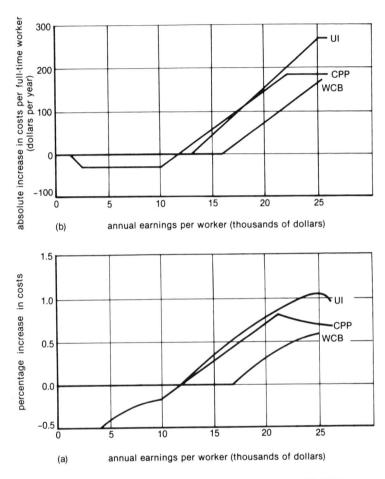

(b)   annual earnings per worker (thousands of dollars)

(a)   annual earnings per worker (thousands of dollars)

Figure 5   The effect of jobsharing on company contributions to UI, CPP, and Workmen's Compensation

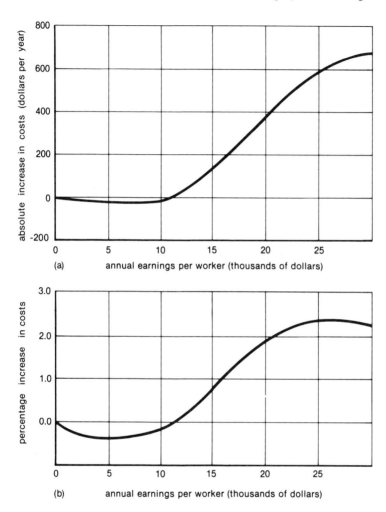

Figure 6   The effect of jobsharing on contribution costs: sum of UI, Workmen's Compensation, and health insurance

Finally, jobsharing has some significant advantages that could reduce labour costs. Studies of actual jobsharing situations indicate that productivity often rises because the jobsharing employees bring more energy and enthusiasm to the job (Meier 1979). Another important advantage is that during periods when one jobsharer is absent due to vacation, illness, or normal turnover the 'partner' can increase hours of work to prevent a serious disruption. Advantages are also apparent in the training of new employees and in giving the employer more flexibility in responding to peak work periods.

To summarize: simulation analysis indicated that worksharing would produce a small increase in labour costs because of fringe benefits, which could easily be more than offset by a reduction in replacement costs. Jobsharing produces a more substantial increase in costs due to fringe benefits and an additional increase in costs due to replacement costs. Jobsharing also has some important advantages which could offset part or all of these cost increases. At the present time, however, those advantages do not seem to be widely recognized by employers since jobsharing has not been widely implemented.

3
The implications of employment-sharing for workers

The factors that determine the number of hours a person is prepared to work are very important in considering the possibility of employment-sharing from the perspective of labour supply. In this section we shall summarize the findings of current economic theory on this question and explain their implications.

A crucial element in the theory of hours of work is the use of what are termed indifference curves. An indifference curve represents the level of satisfaction that a person derives from consuming various combinations of two commodities. For the purposes of this study we shall assume that the two commodities that contribute to a worker's satisfaction are income and leisure time. By leisure time we mean those hours not devoted to income-producing work.

Figure 7 shows three indifference curves, I_0, I_1, and I_2. Each curve represents a level of satisfaction that can be obtained by various combinations of income and leisure. The level of satisfaction represented by every point on any given indifference curve is the same. For example, points B and C in Figure 7 represent the same level of satisfaction, I_0. At point B an employee works forty-seven hours in return for E_2 income; at point C, an equal level of satisfaction is obtained by working forty-one hours for E_1 income. At point B the employee sacrifices six

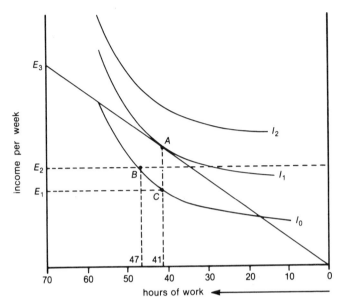

Figure 7 Equilibrium

Each of the three indifference curves in this figure (I_0, I_1, and I_2) represents a level
of satisfaction that a worker can achieve by different combinations of income (E)
and leisure (i.e. all time not spent in wage-earning work). The level of satisfaction
obtained from every point on any given curve is the same. Thus, points B and C on
indifference curve I_0 represent the same level of satisfaction, even though they are
achieved by combining different amounts of E and leisure. The worker will be
equally satisfied at points B and C, and he is therefore indifferent between these
two possible combinations of E and leisure.
   The worker's budget line, OE_3, shows the total amount of income that he would
earn for each total number of hours he works each week at the given wage. When
the budget line is combined with the worker's indifference curves it is possible to
demonstrate a worker's preference for income and leisure at a given wage. Since
it is assumed that a worker will always consume leisure and income in such a way
as to achieve the highest possible level of satisfaction, the indifference curve that
is tangent to the budget line shows the precise combination of income and leisure
that the worker will choose if given the opportunity to do so. Indifference curve I_1
in the above figure is tangent to the budget line at point A. This point is therefore
the point of equilibrium for this worker under these circumstances, and economic
theory predicts that the worker would choose the combination of E and leisure
necessary to achieve this point.

hours of leisure to obtain E_2-E_1 *more* income; at point C the worker
sacrifices E_2-E_1 income to gain six hours *more* leisure time. Since the
levels of satisfaction at B and C are the same, the worker may be said to
be *indifferent* between these two combinations of income and leisure.

Different levels of satisfaction are achieved, of course, if different total quantities of the two commodities are obtained. Higher levels of satisfaction are represented by indifference curves that are higher and to the right. In Figure 7, indifference curve I_1 represents a higher level of satisfaction than I_0, and I_2 represents a higher level than I_1, because at each higher level a worker will have more income for the same number of hours of work, or more leisure time (i.e. *less* work) for the same income, or some compromise between the two. Since indifference curves are a theoretical device representing levels of satisfaction from combinations of two commodities, an infinite number of indifference curves representing an infinite number of possible levels of satisfaction can be constructed for each set of commodities.

In analysing labour supply, however, we are interested in finding the exact number of hours a week that a person will actually want to work at a given hourly wage. To do this we must add to Figure 7 the individual's 'budget line,' OE_3. This line shows the total amount of income that a worker would earn for each number of hours of work each week at the given hourly wage.[1] When the budget line is combined with the indifference curve it becomes possible to demonstrate what a given worker's preference for income and leisure will be at a given wage. We are able to do this by assuming that a worker will always prefer to consume the two commodities (i.e. leisure and income) in such a way as to achieve the *highest possible* level of satisfaction. Point A in Figure 7 clearly satisfies these criteria. Indifference curve I_1, which is tangent to the budget line, represents the highest level of satisfaction (i.e. the highest indifference curve) that can be attained by a combination of income and leisure available at the given wage rate. Indifference curve I_2 represents a higher theoretically possible level of satisfaction for the worker in question, but it can be reached only by a set of combinations of leisure and income unattainable at the given wage rate. Indifference curve I_0 represents a level of satisfaction lower than that attainable at the given wage rate (note that the budget line is above a large portion of I_0). Since the worker is assumed to maximize his satisfaction, this

---

1 The amount of income that can be earned is found by multiplying the wage rate by the number of hours worked each week.

indifference curve is irrelevant. He can do better at point A, and given this wage rate and this set of indifference curves economic theory predicts that the worker in question will choose to work the number of hours and accept the total income available at that point.

A change in the wage rate will produce a change in the number of hours the individual will prefer to work, as we note below. The wage rate is determined by the interaction of demand and supply for all workers in a particular occupation or area. It is assumed that the actions of any one individual will not affect the wage rate, but that the actions of the workers as a whole, represented collectively by a union or association, *can* alter the wage rate.

Six observations follow from the preceding theoretical framework. First, given the wage rate, the condition of the economy, the employees' responsibilities toward their families, and their preferences for varying amounts of income and leisure, employees will prefer to work a certain number of hours a week — for example, forty-one in the case of Figure 7.

Second, even if employees are working the preferred number of hours at current wage rates, they will still be prepared to work overtime if higher wage rates are paid for overtime hours. In the case shown in Figure 8 the higher overtime rate will increase the preferred number of hours of work to forty-three.

Third, if the wage rate for every hour of work were increased, the optimum number of hours would increase or decrease according to individual preference patterns.[2] Figure 9 shows that if an employee's pay is raised so that his budget line rises, he may actually choose to work fewer hours each week. This is what eventually happens when wage rates are increased beyond a certain point, because persons want to spend some of their additional income on increased leisure-time activities.

2 Economists identify an income and a substitution effect when wage rates are changed. The income effect leads to a reduction in the number of hours of work when income is increased. The substitution effect leads to an increase in the number of hours, because when wages are increased the 'cheaper' element (work) is substituted for the 'more expensive' element (leisure). The point at which the number of hours of work decreases when wages increase is the point at which the income effect has grown stronger than the substitution effect.

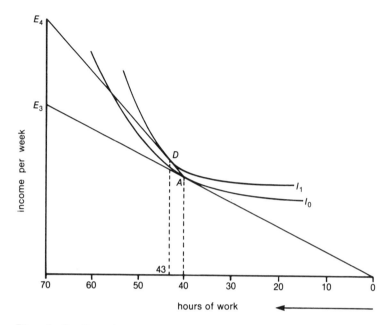

Figure 8   Overtime rate

This figure shows how a higher overtime rate will induce workers to supply more hours of labour to an employer. If the standard wage rate is offered for all hours of work, the worker is in equilibrium at point A on indifference curve I_0 at the normal work-week of 40 hours. If the rate is increased for work beyond the normal 40 hours the budget line is adjusted to rise more steeply to the left of point A, because more income will be received for each hour of work. This altered budget line is no longer tangent to indifference curve I_0; it is tangent to I_1, which represents a higher level of satisfaction. The worker in question will therefore *prefer* to work more hours and receive more income at his new equilibrium, point D.

Fourth, an increase in non-employment income will normally lead to a decrease in the number of hours of labour that will be supplied if the wage rate is unchanged (see Figure 10).[3]

Fifth, if the wage rate and other working conditions are equal between two firms, an employee will prefer to work for the firm that

3 Throughout our analysis it is assumed that leisure and income are normal goods. In the case of leisure this means that people prefer not to work and must receive income in exchange for the leisure hours they give up.

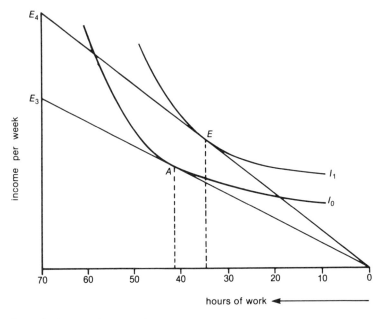

Figure 9   Increase in wage rates

This figure shows how an increase in the rate of pay can cause a worker to desire more leisure time. At the original wage rate the worker is in equilibrium at point A on indifference curve I_0. But the wage increase establishes a new budget line, E_4, which is tangent to a higher indifference curve, I_1, at point E. For the worker in question point E is achieved by a combination of leisure and income that involves working *fewer* hours and taking more leisure time. A wage increase will therefore induce this particular worker to supply less of his labour to the employer.

specifies a work week most closely corresponding to his own preference. Thus, firms have an incentive to adjust the length of their work week to suit the preferences of their employees in order to attract and retain their work force.

Sixth, when there is a limitation on the number of hours that a person can work two phenomena may result: (a) he may be working fewer hours than he prefers; or (b) he may be working more hours than he prefers.

Phenomenon (a) occurs when a person wants to work extra hours at the current wage rate but the employer is unwilling or unable to pay for

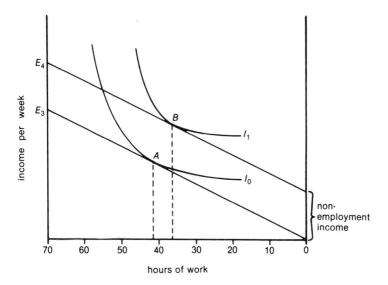

Figure 10   Increase in non-employment income

This figure shows how an increase in non-employment income will always reduce the number of hours of labour that a worker will be willing to supply. Without the non-employment income the worker is in equilibrium at point A on indifference curve I_0 and is working the normal 40-hour week. When he receives non-employment income a new budget line, E_4, is established parallel to his original budget line. The new budget line is tangent to a higher indifference curve, I_1, at point B, which is the worker's new equilibrium *with* the non-employment income. Under these circumstances the worker will supply fewer hours of labour.

any extra hours (Figure 11). The employee is not being hired for as many hours as he wants at the given wage rate; the number of hours of work he is offered gives him a lower level of satisfaction than might otherwise be obtained. Under these circumstances he may seek additional work outside the firm, a practice commonly called moonlighting. Such work may be performed at a lower wage than that paid by the main employer.

An employee may also decide to moonlight even when he is working the desired number of hours at the going wage rate, if he is offered additional work by another employer at wages above the current rate. Such an offer is similar to a higher wage rate for overtime work. In both

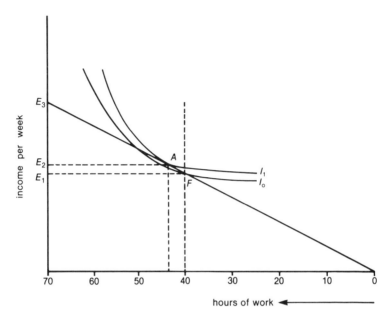

Figure 11 Underemployment

This figure shows how a worker can be underemployed at a given wage rate. The worker in question is in equilibrium at point *A* on indifference curve I_0; that is, if he were given the opportunity to work as much as he wanted at the given wage rate he would choose to work *over* 40 hours a week. But his employer limits him to 40 hours a week, and since the worker cannot obtain the same level of satisfaction working 40 hours a week at that wage rate as he could obtain by working *more* than 40 hours a week (i.e. indifference curve I_0 is not tangent to the budget line at this point), he must settle for a lower level of satisfaction (and therefore a lower indifference curve). Indifference curve I_1, which is below I_0, passes through point *F*. It is this combination of income and leisure that the worker must accept.

cases working the extra hours (whether in the firm or outside it) is a response to the higher wage rate for these additional hours.

A limitation on the number of hours of work available can produce phenomenon (b), where an employee would prefer to work fewer hours than are offered at the standard rate but is given an 'all-or-nothing' choice – he must either work full-time or leave his job (Figure 12). If he works the required number of hours he will do so at a lower level of

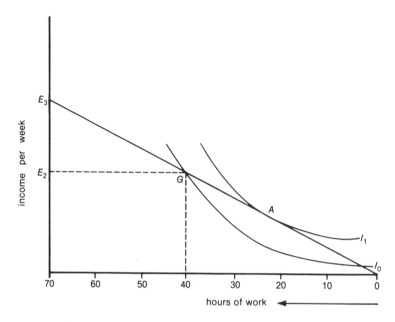

Figure 12 Overemployment

This figure shows how a worker can be overemployed at a given wage rate. The worker in question is in equilibrium at point A on indifference curve I_0; that is, if he were given the opportunity to work as much as he wanted at the given wage rate he would choose to work fewer than 40 hours a week. But his employer requires him to work a full 40-hour work-week, and since the worker cannot obtain the same level of satisfaction working 40 hours a week at that wage rate as he could obtain by working *fewer* than 40 hours a week (i.e. indifference curve I_0 is not tangent to the budget line at this point), he must settle for a lower level of satisfaction (and therefore a lower indifference curve). Indifference curve I_1, which is below I_0, passes through point G. It is this combination of income and leisure that the worker must accept.

satisfaction. If an employee has the opportunity to work at substantially higher rates than the primary employment offers he may want to reduce the number of hours in his primary employment and increase the number of hours in his secondary employment (Bollman 1978).

There is no reason to assume that everyone will prefer to work the same number of hours at a given wage rate. A variety of factors will determine an individual's preferences, (i.e. the shape of his indifference curves) including the size of his family, the role of the person in the family, how many other wage earners are in the family, his age, his geographic location, his level of education, etc. These factors and a number of others are discussed in more detail in the following section.

FACTORS THAT AFFECT THE WILLINGNESS OF WORKERS TO SHARE EMPLOYMENT

The previous section suggests that workers who are overemployed in their current jobs (i.e. those who would prefer to work fewer hours than the standard work week) are most likely to support employment-sharing. This implies that we can predict an employee's attitude toward employment-sharing by examining the labour-supply factors that affect the strength of his attachment to the labour force.[4]

In the discussion below we shall draw on the theory of labour supply to formulate several hypotheses regarding the factors determining an employee's preferences for worksharing. The reader should bear in mind that here we are considering the effect each factor has by itself, other things being equal. In any real-life application many factors will be relevant simultaneously, and it will be necessary to consider their effects in combination.

A worker may be unwilling to support employment-sharing for various reasons. If he has an extremely interesting job, for example, he is less likely to agree to reduce the number of hours he devotes to it each week than one who does not. Similarly, a worker who will effectively be penalized under employment-sharing by fringe benefit provisions will probably resist any attempt to adopt such a scheme. If laid off workers find other jobs that offer attractive pay, high status, a good geographical location, and long-term career opportunities readily available, the desire to share employment will be reduced; the availability of

---

4 For ease of exposition we shall designate a person who desires to work a relatively large number of hours through most or all of the year as one who has a 'permanent' or 'strong' attachment to the labour force, and we shall designate someone who prefers to work relatively few hours through most or all of the year as one who has a 'temporary' or 'weak' attachment to the labour force.

good UI benefits and a short waiting period for the receipt of these benefits can have the same effect. Finally, social and cultural attitudes of varying kinds can influence a worker to reject employment-sharing. If, for example, an individual's self-esteem and status depend on the amount of paid employment he undertakes, he may oppose work-sharing because it threatens his social position.

Many factors can also reinforce the desire for worksharing. Workers directly threatened by a layoff, especially if it is expected to be lengthy and if UI benefits are thought to be inadequate, will naturally tend to support employment-sharing. Even those not threatened by a layoff, however, may support employment-sharing if UI benefits are used to compensate them for lost wages[5] or if the reduction in hours resulting from employment-sharing allows them to earn more by moonlighting. Support for employment-sharing will also probably be stronger among unionized workers who have a well-developed feeling of solidarity; in such cases even workers who are not threatened by layoffs may agree to share employment for the sake of their fellows.

A worker's preference for work and leisure, and thus his attitude towards employment-sharing, will also vary according to a number of personal characteristics. These characteristics include, besides personal tastes, the worker's financial responsibilities, size of family, personal wealth, age, and sex. Age and sex are especially important variables in this particular study, because they are the main labour force character-istics for which data are consistently available. For this reason we have chosen age and sex categories as crude proxies to estimate the degree of attachment of workers to the labour force. In the next chapter we shall undertake some empirical tests of our employment-sharing model using these variables to predict the incidence of employment-sharing in various industries. A few words about the significance of these cate-gories are therefore in order here.

We have divided employees into three age categories: prime-age workers (25 to 54 years old), young workers (those under 25), and older workers (those 55 and over). Since the average prime-age worker has more family responsibilities than his younger or older counterpart, we expect that prime-age workers will prefer to work more hours each

5 This possibility is examined in detail in Chapter 5.

year and be less inclined towards employment-sharing than those in either of the other two groups. Though a sizable proportion of working women have a strong attachment to the labour force either because they are heads of households or because they are committed to careers, the proportion of working men with a strong attachment to the labour force remains even larger. We thus expect that a group with a high proportion of female employees will be more inclined towards employment-sharing than one with a high proportion of male employees.

FACTORS THAT CAN AFFECT UNION RESPONSES TO PROPOSALS FOR EMPLOYMENT-SHARING

A union reflects the desires of its members as individuals and has its own objectives as an institution. It can comprise a mixture of groups with different degrees of attachment to the labour force, and it may have to consider various other factors as well: e.g. its organizational structure, the nature of its leadership, competition with other unions, the economic conditions facing the industry or industries involved, employment prospects for the union's members, and general economic conditions. All these forces interact to determine the response of a union or of a particular union local to the possibility of employment-sharing.

The factors that can lead a union to favour employment-sharing are these:

— a predominance of older workers among its members;
— the use of worksharing to reduce unemployment among union and non-union members in a bargaining unit;
— the use of jobsharing to increase employment for union members;
— the use of worksharing and jobsharing to provide greater flexibility of hours for workers wanting to work less than full-time; and
— the use of jobsharing to provide opportunities for non-union workers to acquire skills and thereby join unions with skilled workers, thus increasing the potential membership of the union.

Factors that tend to deter a union from accepting employment-sharing are as follows:

— the presence of a large number of prime-age union members with a permanent attachment to the labour force;

— the fear of an increase in the divisions between groups within the union as a result of worksharing (Sadlier-Brown 1978);

— the view that worksharing may permit a perpetuation of lower incomes by permitting employees to work fewer hours, possibly at unchanged rates of pay;

— the fear that worksharing will reduce the pressure for wage increases, since persons who otherwise might have been laid off will be reluctant to press too vigorously for increases in wages and benefits;

— the suspicion that jobsharing will reduce the union's ability to press for wage increases because of the inclusion of part-time persons with a lesser long-term commitment to the job;

— the perception that worksharing reduces productivity incentives and thereby reduces the ability of the company to raise wages;

— the fear that jobsharing may require a union to reapply for certification for a new unit including both part-time and full-time employees; at present the Ontario Labour Relations Board places part-time employees in separate bargaining units (Weeks 1978);

— the fear that part-time workers may be more difficult to organize than full-time workers; and

— the fear that worksharing deprives some workers of exercising seniority rights and that this might lead to the loss of seniority privileges in other areas.[6]

The schedule of union dues may or may not favour employment-sharing. If union members who are employed part-time still pay full union dues, the union will tend to encourage worksharing and jobsharing. If union members who are employed part-time pay reduced dues, employment-sharing may reduce total union income, and the union may accordingly tend to discourage it.

The combination of the factors outlined above will determine the attitude of each union or union local towards employment-sharing.

6 This consideration was suggested by Henry Koschitsky, president of IKO Industries Ltd, one of the firms which participated in CEIC's worksharing experiment.

4

The test of an economic model of employment-sharing

Chapters 2 and 3 examined employment-sharing theoretically from the different perspectives of employers and employees. This chapter tries to isolate those economic circumstances favourable to employment-sharing when both demand and supply are taken into account. In addition, we shall bring forward data from past experiences with two varieties of employment-sharing and use these data to test our theoretical model. The first is the incidence of worksharing provisions in collective agreements by industry, and the second is the demographic pattern of part-time employment.

DEMAND AND SUPPLY FACTORS

In Chapter 2 we analysed the factors that influence an employer's decision about whether to employ one person full-time or to employ several persons less than full-time. The following three factors were found to encourage employment-sharing: (a) a system that bases employer contributions to fringe benefits wholly or largely on the number of hours of labour rather than the number of employees; (b) a work force in which each individual worker has a narrow range of skills and training; and (c) low costs for the recruitment, training, and administration of personnel.[1] In Chapter 3 we suggested that young workers, older workers, and other persons with a more temporary

_____

1 We can expect factor (c) to be associated with jobs earning lower average wages.

attachment to the labour force would be most likely to accept employment-sharing. This suggestion was based on a consideration of their most likely alternative interests and activities. The observations from these two chapters form the basis for a general model that can be tested with actual data on employment-sharing.

WORKSHARING PROVISIONS IN COLLECTIVE AGREEMENTS

We tested the employment-sharing model by comparing the incidence of worksharing provisions in collective agreements in Ontario in August 1978 with the predictions made from our model. The data base includes all collective agreements in public administration and all other collective agreements in Ontario covering two hundred or more employees in a bargaining unit. The total sample is 2163 collective agreements in Ontario covering a total of 816,172 employees in thirty-six industry groups.

An agreement was deemed to have a worksharing provision if it included one or more of the following:

− a provision to reduce the regular hours of work in order to minimize layoffs when there is insufficient work to continue to employ all regular employees for a full work week;
− a provision that, where piece rates are in effect, layoffs are minimized by spreading the available work among all employees;
− a provision to stop employers from scheduling overtime during slack periods until all laid-off employees have been recalled.

Of the 816,172 employees and 2163 agreements in the sample 7.6 per cent (61,934) of the employees were covered by worksharing provisions and 6.2 per cent (135) of the agreements contained such provisions (Table 7). The most common worksharing provision is the reduction of regular hours (5.7 per cent of the employees), next is the spreading of piecework (2.7 per cent of the employees), and third is the restriction of overtime (1.2 per cent of the employees).[2] The frequency of worksharing provisions varied strikingly from one industry to

2 These figures add to more than 7.6 per cent because some collective agreements contain more than one of the three provisions.

TABLE 7
Worksharing provisions in collective agreements in Ontario

Industry	(1) Number of employees	(2) Percentage of employees worksharing	(3) Average weekly earnings of wage earners ($)	(4) Percentage of female employees	(5) Percentage of employees part-time (Canada)	(6) Percentage of employees in prime age (25 to 24) (Ontario)
Forestry	4,935	0.0	326.88	2.0	5.1	66.2
Mines and quarries	26,114	1.0	329.74	5.5	1.5	66.2
Food and beverage	21,929	14.8	251.32	28.3	6.1	64.1
Tobacco product	1,607	0.0	289.14	31.8	1.1	69.9
Rubber industry	9,610	19.4	251.61	19.4	2.3	69.0
Leather industry	3,297	44.3	174.02	60.2	3.5	60.2
Textile industry	10,925	13.7	226.01	42.0	1.9	65.6
Knitting mills	1,125	33.8	155.91	74.5	3.5	60.6
Clothing industry	7,836	97.1	158.33	74.3	4.5	63.8
Wood industry	3,145	0.0	223.42	15.7	4.0	59.1
Furniture fixtures	3,711	29.9	211.58	27.8	3.5	63.1
Paper-allied	20,801	6.5	311.01	16.7	1.6	67.0
Printing and publishing	6,446	27.1	253.24	36.8	14.7	60.6
Primary metal	31,216	16.8	321.55	6.8	1.1	69.5
Metal fabricating	18,414	9.5	282.13	17.8	2.3	68.3
Machinery industry	13,988	23.6	296.72	12.3	1.5	70.9
Transportation equipment	80,299	3.5	337.68	12.0	1.1	75.2
Electrical production	35,272	10.7	232.29	33.8	1.2	70.3
Non-metallic production	9,196	5.9	296.85	14.4	2.4	68.8
Petroleum and coal	1,518	0.0	366.04	26.3	1.2	70.1
Chemical and production	7,091	0.0	275.07	25.0	2.8	69.2
Miscellaneous manufacturing	6,235	12.6	203.66	42.6	4.2	65.8
Transportation	56,054	1.0	307.83	10.9	5.9	69.5

TABLE 7 continued

Industry	(1) Number of employees	(2) Percentage of employees worksharing	(3) Average weekly earnings of wage earners ($)	(4) Percentage of female employees	(5) Percentage of employees part-time (Canada)	(6) Percentage of employees in prime age (25 to 54) (Ontario)
Storage	1,725	0.0	n.a.	n.a.	7.7	60.4
Communication	29,408	50.2	285.12	36.5	6.6	65.9
Utilities public	23,103	3.3	n.a.	n.a.	2.1	69.5
Wholesale trade	2,188	0.0	266.56	26.1	6.0	54.7
Retail trade	37,271	4.4	172.99	49.7	25.1	54.3
Finance and insurance	965	0.0	254.50	60.6	7.9	60.3
Education services	41,730	4.2	n.a.	n.a.	21.7	67.1
Health and welfare	70,793	2.5	n.a.	n.a.	14.5	61.0
Motion picture	3,366	0.3	n.a.	n.a.	33.5	44.3
Business services and management	5,335	7.9	248.07	40.4	9.2	65.6
Personal service	9,919	5.8	115.90	53.9	28.3	51.9
Miscellaneous services	571	0.0	213.70	33.8	19.8	61.9
Public administration	209,034	0.5	n.a.	n.a.	6.1	55.8
Total/Average	816,172	7.6	n.a.	29.8	11.8	62.4

NOTE: Part-time is defined as working less than thirty hours a week.

SOURCES:

Columns (1) and (2) from a special tabulation provided by the Ontario Ministry of Labour relating to collective agreements in Ontario. Columns (3) and (4) from *Employment and Earnings* (72-002) July 1978, data are for Ontario for June 1978. Data on weekly earnings relate to wage-earners except the following industries for which data were available only for all employees: Forestry, Transportation, Communication, Wholesale trade, Retail trade, Business services, Personal services, Miscellaneous services. Column (5) from 1971 Census of Canada, Labour Force Activity-Work Experience, Cat. 94-783, Vol. III—Part 7, Bulletin 3.7-13 January 1975. Column (6) from 1971 Census of Canada, Industries, Cat. 94-747, Vol. III—Part 4, Bulletin 3.4-10 March 1975.

another: 97.1 per cent of the employees in the clothing manufacturing industry were covered while several industries were found to have no worksharing provisions at all.[3]

In order to test the usefulness of our model in explaining the incidence of worksharing among industries we first present a cursory qualitative test followed by a more formal statistical test using multiple regression analysis.

In our cursory qualitative test we analysed the seven industries with the highest incidence of worksharing (over 20 per cent of the employees) and the eight industries without any worksharing (Table 8). Our analysis in Chapter 2 indicated that the average wage paid in an industry will have an ambiguous effect on the firm's attitude towards worksharing. On the one hand our simulations indicated a small increase in costs when employee earnings reach $12,000 or $13,000 a year (i.e. $230 to $250 a week). On the other hand employees in high-wage industries tend to have more specific human capital, and the costs of replacing and retraining a lost worker would be higher. In such industries the savings from replacement costs would be greater, and firms might be more inclined toward worksharing. For the purpose of this cursory analysis we assumed that the former effect dominates, and we therefore hypothesized that industries which paid weekly salaries below $230 a week would have a high incidence of worksharing (shown as 'H' in Table 8) indicated from demand considerations, that industries in which earnings were above $250 a week would have a low incidence (shown as 'L'), and that industries in which earnings were between $230 and $250 a week would have a middle-range incidence (shown as 'M').

We analysed supply predictors in much the same way. Since females are more willing to workshare than males, we hypothesized that an industry with a high percentage of female employees would have a high incidence of worksharing, that an industry with a low percentage of female employees would have a low incidence, and that an industry with an average percentage of female employees would have a middle-range incidence. The relation between prime-age workers and the

3 Note that for the purpose of our analysis the mere presence of worksharing provisions in collective agreements was deemed sufficient. No attempt was made to find out if these provisions were actually invoked.

TABLE 8

A qualitative analysis of the incidence of worksharing among industries

Industry	Prediction from demand side	Prediction from supply side		Prediction from combined demand and supply	Actual incidence of work sharing
		Percentage female	Percentage prime age		
High worksharing					
Leather	H	H	M	H	H
Knitting	H	H	M	H	H
Clothing	H	H	M	H	H
Furniture	H	M	M	H	H
Printing	M	H	M	H	H
Machinery	L	L	L	L	H
Communication	L	H	L	n.a.	H
Zero worksharing					
Forestry	L	L	L	L	L
Tobacco	L	M	L	L	L
Wood	H	L	H	n.a.	L
Petroleum	L	M	L	L	L
Chemical	L	M	L	L	L
Storage	n.a.	n.a.	M	n.a.	L
Wholesale trade	L	M	H	n.a.	L
Finance	L	H	M	n.a.	L
Miscellaneous services	H	M	M	H	L

NOTE: H indicates a high level of worksharing, L a low level of worksharing, and M a middle-range level of worksharing. 'n.a.' indicates that data were not available for the industry in question, or that a prediction could not be made because the supply and demand effects conflicted and their relative strengths were not known.

incidence of worksharing, also shown in Table 8, was predicted to be the inverse of that for females.[4]

We could not predict the net effect of supply and demand if the data for an industry were unavailable, or if there were both 'H' and 'L'

4 The following boundaries were used:

	High	Medium	Low
Female percentage	over 34.6	34.6 to 25.0	under 25.0
Prime-age percentage	over 64.8	64.8 to 60.0	under 60.0

predictors for an industry. The relative strengths of both supply and demand must be known before their net effect can be predicted. Such results can be obtained with regression coefficients in a statistical analysis, but they are beyond the scope of the qualitative analysis presented here.

In spite of these limitations we were able to predict the net effect of supply and demand in eleven of the sixteen industries. We predicted a high incidence of worksharing in the leather, knitting, clothing, furniture, printing, and miscellaneous industries, and a low incidence of worksharing in the machinery, forestry, tobacco, petroleum, and chemical industries. A comparison of these predictions with the actual incidence of worksharing in these industries shows that our predictions were correct in nine of the eleven cases. We regard this as encouraging support for the theoretical model and an indication that it is capable of explaining at least the gross differences between high worksharing and low worksharing industries.

We turn now to the multiple regression analysis of worksharing incidence by industry. The dependent variable is the number of employees in each industry covered by worksharing provisions as a percentage of total employees in the industry covered by collective agreements (SHARE). The explanatory variables are the average weekly earnings in the industry (WAGE), female employees as a percentage of total employees in the industry (FEMALE), part-time employees as a percentage of total employees in the industry (PART), and the percentage of the industry's employees in the prime-age group (PRIME). All data and the sources are listed in Table 7.

The equation estimated is of the general form

$$\text{SHARE} = b_0 + b_1 \text{ WAGE} + b_2 \text{ FEMALE} + b_3 \text{ PART} + b_4 \text{ PRIME}.$$

As indicated above, the sign of the coefficient b_1 cannot be determined unambiguously from the theoretical discussion of Chapter 2. There is a tendency towards a negative coefficient since in high-wage industries worksharing would result in a greater increase in fringe benefit costs and therefore less worksharing. At the same time there is an offsetting tendency towards a positive coefficient since worksharing generates greater savings in replacement costs in high-wage industries where the costs of training a lost employee tend to be higher.

The analysis in Chapter 3 indicated that, at least in those households where the traditional division of tasks still prevails, women will perform more of the domestic work and therefore will tend to prefer a smaller number of hours of market work than males. Given the prevalence of a standard work week in many industries, many employees are forced to choose between working the standard week or not working at all. This theoretical analysis implies that a higher fraction of employed women will be overemployed than men (i.e. a higher fraction of women will be working more hours than they prefer at the current real wage). Thus we expect the coefficient b_2 to have a positive sign.

Similarly, theoretical analysis suggests that prime-age workers will prefer to work more hours than younger or older workers, other things equal. Thus a smaller proportion of prime-age workers will be over-employed, implying a negative coefficient on the PRIME variable.

In industries where part-time work is prevalent, those employees who wish to work fewer hours than the standard work week will have a greater opportunity to do so. Thus there will be fewer employees who are overemployed and a lower preference for worksharing. From this argument a negative coefficient on PART is expected.

In the statistical analysis those industries for which the information available is incomplete (indicated by 'n.a.' in Table 7) are excluded. Also excluded are those industries which have zero worksharing, to avoid the statistical problems which result when a number of observations of the dependent variable are clustered at a limiting point and to avoid the use of a more specialized regression technique (Tobit analysis).

Tables 9 and 10 present the means and standard deviations for each variable and the correlation matrix. Table 11 presents the results of estimating equation (4.1) using ordinary least squares regression. In the first four equations in that table each explanatory variable is included separately. The FEMALE variable is the most significant statistically and has the expected positive coefficient. The PART and PRIME variables have negative coefficients as expected but are not statistically significant at the 0.05 significance level. The negative coefficient of the WAGE variable suggests that worksharing is more common in low-wage industries.

The picture changes somewhat in equation (5), where all four explanatory variables are included. The FEMALE variable remains the most significant, with a t-statistic of 2.6. The coefficient of the WAGE

TABLE 9
Means and standard deviations

	Mean	Standard deviation
SHARE	20.0	21.4
WAGE	246.5	61.8
FEMALE	32.6	20.2
PART	6.0	7.3
PRIME	65.3	5.3

TABLE 10
Correlation matrix

	SHARE	WAGE	FEMALE	PART	PRIME
SHARE	1.00	-0.40	0.60	-0.12	-0.16
WAGE	-0.40	1.00	-0.90	-0.55	0.80
FEMALE	0.60	-0.90	1.00	0.39	-0.68
PART	-0.12	-0.55	0.39	1.00	-0.82
PRIME	-0.16	0.80	-0.68	-0.82	1.00

variable changes sign and becomes statistically insignificant. The explanation for this result is in Table 10, which indicates a high inverse correlation between the average wage in an industry and the percentage of female employees in the industry ($r = -0.90$). These results indicate that the WAGE variable appeared significant mainly because of the correlation with FEMALE. When the percentage of female employees is held constant (as in the regression analysis) there is very little independent influence of WAGE. This result is consistent with our theoretical analysis, which indicated that the effects on fringe costs are small and may be more than offset by savings in replacement costs. The multiple regression also causes an increase in the significance of the PART variable and a decrease in the significance of PRIME.

Equation (6) of Table 11 is our preferred regression result. It shows that an increase in FEMALE increases the tendency toward worksharing, and an increase in PART decreases the tendency toward worksharing. Both those results are consistent with our theoretical analysis and statistically significant. The R^2 indicates that two variables are able to explain approximately one-half of the total variation in the incidence of worksharing provisions among industries.

TABLE 11

Regression analysis of the incidence of worksharing among industries

Equation	Constant	WAGE	FEMALE	PART	PRIME	R^2
1	54.20	−0.14				0.16
	(3.0)	(−2.0)				
2	−0.59		0.63			0.36
	(−0.1)		(3.3)			
3	22.08			−0.35		0.01
	(3.6)			(−0.5)		
4	61.68				−0.63	0.02
	(1.0)				(−0.7)	
5	−36.57	0.13	1.12	−1.01	−0.11	0.52
	(−0.3)	(0.8)	(2.6)	(−1.1)	(−0.1)	
6	1.18		0.80	−1.22		0.50
	(0.2)	0.80	(4.3)	(−2.4)		

NOTE: t-statistics in parentheses; R^2 is the coefficient of multiple determination.

PATTERNS OF PART-TIME EMPLOYMENT

Part-time employment is the most widespread of all types of employ-ment-sharing, and it provides the most complete data base. In this section we shall discuss five aspects of part-time employment in Ontario and Canada: age-sex differences,[5] reasons for working part-time, occu-pations and industries, wage and salary rates, and unemployment rates.

Age-sex differences

Table 12 shows the historical trend in the incidence of part-time work in Ontario.[6] Between 1966 and 1975 the proportion of employed

5 In Chapter 3 we discussed the effect that a person's age and attachment to the labour force have on his willingness to share employment. Unfortunately, data on attachment to the labour force as such are not available. In this section we discuss part-time work using age and sex categories as crude proxies for the degree of labour-force attachment. Historical data indicate that prime-age males were much more permanently attached to the labour force than prime-age females. This trend is clearly changing, but since our only data source indicates age and sex we shall use it to give a general overview of trends in part-time employment.

6 Before 1975 part-time work was defined as work that consumed less than thirty-five hours a week. In 1976 the criterion was lowered to thirty hours a week.

males and females who worked part-time increased by almost half from 9.6 to 13.4 per cent. This form of employment-sharing is thus significant and growing. In 1976, under the new definition of part-time work as that requiring less than thirty hours a week, 12.0 per cent of the employed were working part-time. The proportion of part-time workers was far higher among females than among males: in 1976 the rate was 22.3 per cent for females and only 5.7 per cent for males.

The incidence of part-time work differed from one age group to another (Table 13). The highest rates were experienced by young workers and the lowest by prime-age workers. Among the males the differences were very striking: 19.3 per cent of the young males and 2.0 per cent of the prime-age males were employed part-time. The comparable figures for females in 1973 are 26.3 and 21.8 per cent respectively. Older workers experienced the second-highest incidence of part-time work; the rate among older females was nearly as high as that among young females, but among older males it was only slightly above that of prime-age males.

Data from the United States show the same patterns, though the overall incidence of part-time work is higher. In 1975, 22.4 per cent of employed Americans and only 13.3 per cent of employed Canadians were working part-time. In May 1977 the proportion of persons voluntarily working part-time by sex and age in the United States was as shown in Table 14 (Deutermann and Brown 1978). The patterns in the incidence of part-time employment are consistent with the predictions made in Chapter 3.

Reasons for working part-time
In the April 1977 Labour Force Survey persons working part-time were asked their reasons for doing so. The main reasons they gave for working part-time were a desire not to work full-time and attendance at school. As Table 15 shows, this pattern prevailed both in Ontario and in Canada as a whole. Among young workers in Canada attendance at school is the most important reason for working part-time (69.5 per cent), and among older workers a desire not to work full-time is the most important reason (66.1 per cent). Of the prime-age males who were working part-time, 27.3 per cent said they were doing so because they could find only part-time work, and another 21.2 per cent said they did not want to work full-time; only 10.2 per cent of the prime-age females were working part-time because they could find no full-

TABLE 12

Percentage of employed males and females who were working part-time, Ontario, 1966-76 (thousands)

Year	Both sexes			Males			Females		
	Total employed	Number part-time	Percentage part-time	Total employed	Number part-time	Percentage part-time	Total employed	Number part-time	Percentage part-time
1966	2651	254	9.6	1820	73	4.0	830	181	21.8
1967	2745	273	9.9	1864	85	4.6	881	188	21.3
1968	2830	304	10.7	1910	91	4.8	920	212	23.0
1969	2936	335	11.4	1965	100	5.1	972	235	24.2
1970	2996	364	12.1	1993	115	5.8	1002	249	24.9
1971	3079	379	12.3	2021	118	5.8	1058	261	24.7
1972	3218	395	12.3	2099	123	5.9	1119	271	24.2
1973	3366	405	12.0	2179	121	5.6	1187	284	23.9
1974	3519	435	12.4	2257	127	5.6	1261	309	24.5
1975	3581	479	13.4	2268	n.a.	n.a.	1313	n.a.	n.a.
1975	3613	431	11.9	2248	132	5.9	1364	299	21.9
1976	3689	444	12.0	2279	129	5.7	1410	315	22.3

NOTE: Up to 1975 part-time work was defined to include those persons who usually work less than thirty-five hours a week and considered themselves to be working part-time. From 1975 on part-time work was defined to include those who work less than thirty hours a week. A change in the definition of 'employed' in the Labour Force Survey accounts for differences in the total employed for 1975.

SOURCE: Robertson (1976, Tables 1, 3, and 4)

TABLE 13

TABLE 13
Distribution of employed labour force working part-time by sex and age, Ontario, Annual Averages, 1966 and 1973

	1966 Number (000)	1966 %	1973 Number (000)	1973 %	Percentage change 1966 to 1973	Part-time to total employment ratios 1966 1966	Part-time to total employment ratios 1973 1973
Male							
14-24	47	18.5	87	21.5	85.1	14.5	19.3
25-44	5	2.0	9	2.2	80.0	0.6	0.9
45 & over	21	8.3	25	6.2	19.0	3.2	3.5
Total	73	28.7	121	29.9	65.8	4.0	5.6
Female							
14-24	39	15.4	90	22.2	130.8	17.0	26.3
25-44	82	32.3	109	26.9	32.9	23.9	21.8
45 & over	60	23.6	85	21.0	41.7	23.3	24.7
Total	181	71.3	284	70.1	56.9	21.8	23.9
Both							
14-24	86	33.9	177	43.7	105.8	15.5	22.3
25-44	87	34.3	118	29.1	35.6	7.3	7.9
45 & over	81	31.9	110	27.2	35.8	8.9	10.3
Total	254	100.0	405	100.0	59.4	9.6	12.0

SOURCE: Robertson (1976, 11)

TABLE 14
Proportion of persons voluntarily working part-
time in the United States, May 1977

	Men	Women
16 years and over	7.6	22.7
16 to 24 years	25.2	30.9
16 to 19 years	50.4	55.9
20 to 24 years	10.8	16.8
25 to 54 years	1.5	18.6
55 to 64 years	2.8	19.4
65 years and over	39.3	54.3

time work, and 58.3 per cent said they were not interested in working full-time.

Occupations and industries
Tables 16 and 17 show the occupation and industry distributions of part-time workers in Ontario in both 1966 and 1973. Sales occupations had the highest percentage of part-time workers in 1973, and service occupations had the second highest. The data for Canada as a whole show, however, that the proportion of part-time male workers was greater in service occupations than in sales occupations, which ranked second (see *The Labour Force*, April 1977). In addition, a very large proportion of the employees in the primary industries (i.e. agriculture, forestry, fishing, mining) worked part-time. The trade and service industries had the highest percentages of part-time workers among industry groups. Similar occupation and industry patterns have been reported to occur in the United States (Deutermann and Brown 1978).

Wage and salary rates
Data are not readily available on the earnings of part-time workers in Canada, but since the occupation and industry patterns in Canada are similar to those in the United States, one may assume that similar wage patterns are likely to prevail as well. Owen (1978, 12-13) offers several reasons why part-time workers in the United States tend to be in low-wage jobs:

First, employers are unwilling to make large initial expenditures in screening and training new part-time employees, investments that are required for many high-paid jobs ... Second, high-paid jobs are often

TABLE 15
Reasons for part-time employment in Ontario, and for Canada, by age and sex, annual average for 1976

Age groups by years	Thousands						Percentage					
	Total	Personal or family responsibilities	Going to school	Could only find part-time work	Did not want full-time work	Other reasons	Total	Personal or family responsibilities	Going to school	Could only find part-time work	Did not want full-time work	Other reasons
ONTARIO												
Both sexes	444	49	161	45	172	18	100.0	11.0	36.3	10.1	38.7	4.1
CANADA												
Both sexes	1051	134	353	126	387	51	100.0	12.8	33.6	12.0	36.8	4.9
14-24	491	13	341	66	62	8	100.0	2.7	69.5	13.4	12.6	1.6
25-54	436	107	12	50	242	25	100.0	24.5	2.8	11.5	55.5	5.7
55+	124	13	–	11	82	18	100.0	10.5	0.0	8.9	66.1	14.5
Men	308	4	184	40	55	26	100.0	1.3	59.7	13.0	17.9	8.4
15-24	228	–	177	27	19	4	100.0	0.0	77.6	11.8	8.3	1.8
25-54	33	–	7	9	7	10	100.0	0.0	21.2	27.3	21.2	30.3
55+	46	–	–	4	28	12	100.0	0.0	0.0	8.7	60.9	26.1
Women	743	130	169	87	332	26	100.0	17.5	22.8	11.7	44.7	3.5
15-24	263	12	164	39	43	4	100.0	4.6	62.4	14.8	16.4	1.5
25-54	403	106	5	41	235	15	100.0	26.3	1.2	10.2	58.3	3.7
55+	78	12	–	6	54	6	100.0	15.4	0.0	7.7	69.2	7.7

NOTE: Figures may not add to 100 per cent because of rounding.
SOURCE: Robertson (1976, Table 11), *Labour Force*, April 1977, Table 6

TABLE 16
Distribution of employed labour force working part-time by occupation, annual averages, Ontario, 1966 and 1973

	1966		1973		Percentage change 1966 to 1973	Part-time workers as a percentage of total employment	
	Number (000)	%	Number (000)	%		1966	1973
Professional	29	11.4	47	11.6	62.1	8.7	9.5
Clerical	49	19.3	91	22.5	85.7	11.6	15.8
Sales	43	16.9	74	18.3	72.1	24.0	30.1
Service	69	27.2	109	26.9	58.0	25.2	28.8
Craftsman	14	5.5	24	5.9	71.4	1.9	2.6
Labourers	12	4.7	14	3.5	16.7	9.3	12.1
Other	37	14.6	46	11.4	24.3	6.8	7.1
Total	254	100.0	405	100.0	59.4	9.6	12.0

NOTE: 'Other' includes such occupations as transportation, farming, and other primary.
SOURCE: Robertson (1976, 15)

TABLE 17
Distribution of employed labour force working part-time by industry, annual averages, Ontario, 1966 and 1973

	1966		1973		Percentage change 1966 to 1973	Part-time workers as a percentage of total employment	
	Number (000)	%	Number (000)	%		1966	1973
Manufacturing	23	9.1	32	7.9	39.1	2.8	3.4
Trade	73	28.7	122	30.1	67.1	17.6	22.2
Services	107	42.1	176	43.5	64.5	18.6	20.7
All others	51	20.1	75	18.5	47.1	6.1	7.2
Total	254	100.0	405	100.0	59.4	9.6	12.0

SOURCE: Robertson (1976, 16)

complicated, and found in complex organizational settings, so that supervisory, coordination and communication costs are also high ... Third, changing from full-time to part-time work may only double the size of the direct labour force, without increasing total hours of direct labour.

An additional reason for the relatively low wages of part-time workers is that the supply of potential part-time workers has been growing more rapidly than the capacity of managers to use them, and it is this oversupply that keeps relative wages down.

Unemployment rates for persons seeking part-time work
Before 1975 the number of persons seeking part-time work was small, averaging between 6 and 7 per cent of all unemployed. While the change in the definition of the labour force in 1976 reduced the proportion of employed persons defined as part-time workers, it almost doubled the proportion of the unemployed who were seeking part-time work to 12 per cent (see *The Labour Force*, December 1975 and April 1977).

In Canada as a whole in 1976 the unemployment rate for persons seeking part-time work was greater than that for persons seeking full-time work (7.7 and 6.2 per cent respectively). The reason for this is that the unemployment rate for males seeking part-time work was almost twice that of males seeking full-time work (8.9 and 5.5 per cent respectively). The unemployment rate for females seeking part-time work, however, was less than that for females seeking full-time work.

A further examination of the data shows that the high unemployment rate among males seeking part-time work did not occur among young males, who have the highest overall unemployment rate. Additional analysis is needed to determine whether it is the older male workers or the prime-age males who are responsible for the high incidence of unemployment among prospective part-time workers.

5
The implications for government policies

This chapter considers the advantages and disadvantages of employment-sharing for employers, employees, and society as a whole. We begin by considering projections of the composition of the labour force in Ontario to 1987 and deriving the implications of these projections for the future of employment-sharing. We then discuss the implications of our study for government policy regarding each of the three types of employment-sharing: worksharing, jobsharing, and part-time employment. We conclude with some suggestions for further research.

CHANGES IN THE AGE AND SEX DISTRIBUTION OF THE LABOUR FORCE TO 1987

Three observations can be made about projections for the Ontario labour force during the 1980s shown in Table 18: first, the proportion of females will continue to increase; secondly, the proportion and even the actual number of young persons in the labour force will decrease; and thirdly the number and proportion of workers in the prime-age groups will increase.

Our hypothesis suggests that these predicted changes will have the following implications for the supply of persons willing to engage in employment-sharing: the relative and absolute decrease in younger workers will tend to reduce the supply of persons who wish to work part-time, and this trend is most likely to be more than offset by an

TABLE 18
The Ontario labour force, 1977-87

	1976	1977	1978	1979	1980	1981	1982	1983	1984	1985	1986	1987
Distribution in millions												
Males, total	2.420	2.480	2.534	2.588	2.642	2.695	2.746	2.793	2.839	2.881	2.917	2.954
15 to 19	0.232	0.236	0.240	0.244	0.247	0.245	0.243	0.235	0.228	0.223	0.219	0.220
20 to 24	0.314	0.325	0.336	0.344	0.351	0.360	0.367	0.374	0.379	0.380	0.374	0.368
25 to 44	1.100	1.135	1.164	1.198	1.236	1.273	1.312	1.351	1.391	1.429	1.469	1.501
45 to 64	0.712	0.720	0.728	0.734	0.739	0.746	0.752	0.760	0.768	0.772	0.777	0.785
65 & over	0.062	0.064	0.066	0.068	0.070	0.071	0.072	0.073	0.074	0.076	0.078	0.080
Females, total	1.524	1.571	1.615	1.649	1.695	1.744	1.800	1.848	1.900	1.944	1.985	2.037
15 to 19	0.205	0.208	0.211	0.215	0.218	0.217	0.214	0.208	0.202	0.198	0.196	0.196
20 to 24	0.258	0.266	0.272	0.279	0.285	0.292	0.300	0.306	0.312	0.314	0.309	0.302
25 to 44	0.672	0.702	0.732	0.747	0.778	0.812	0.852	0.890	0.930	0.968	1.010	1.061
45 to 64	0.368	0.375	0.380	0.386	0.392	0.401	0.412	0.422	0.433	0.440	0.445	0.452
65 & over	0.020	0.020	0.021	0.021	0.021	0.022	0.022	0.023	0.024	0.024	0.025	0.026
Distribution in percentages												
Males, total	61.361	61.229	61.073	61.086	60.924	60.703	60.407	60.177	59.907	59.710	59.505	59.189
15 to 19	5.883	5.833	5.786	5.752	5.690	5.520	5.338	5.065	4.821	4.617	4.476	4.411
20 to 24	7.694	8.032	8.091	8.132	8.100	8.109	8.073	8.051	7.987	7.879	7.627	7.368
25 to 44	27.906	28.015	28.057	28.285	28.503	28.682	28.866	29.112	29.342	29.628	29.958	30.078
45 to 64	18.044	17.779	17.553	17.316	17.028	16.800	16.550	16.381	16.195	16.009	15.851	15.725
65 & over	1.563	1.570	1.586	1.602	1.603	1.593	1.579	1.569	1.563	1.576	1.593	1.607
Females, total	38.639	38.771	38.927	38.914	39.076	39.297	39.593	39.823	40.093	40.290	40.495	40.811
15 to 19	5.210	5.128	5.084	5.082	5.029	4.886	4.701	4.483	4.262	4.102	3.997	3.922
20 to 24	6.553	6.567	6.557	6.586	6.574	6.588	6.592	6.592	6.578	6.503	6.303	6.051
25 to 44	17.037	17.338	17.625	17.644	17.942	18.295	18.753	19.164	19.621	20.064	20.607	21.265
45 to 64	9.328	9.248	9.155	9.104	9.035	9.034	9.054	9.088	9.135	9.118	9.076	9.057
65 & over	0.511	0.490	0.497	0.499	0.495	0.494	0.493	0.496	0.497	0.504	0.511	0.517

SOURCE: David K. Foot, James E. Pesando, John A. Sawyer, and John W.C. Winder, *The Ontario Economy, 1977-1987* (Toronto: Ontario Economic Council).

increase in the number of other persons, especially prime-age women, willing to engage in employment-sharing. Furthermore, this change in the age and sex distribution of the labour force is likely to alter the distribution of the occupations and industries toward which the supply of part-time workers and other employment-sharers is directed.

THE POLICY IMPLICATIONS OF THE MODEL FOR WORKSHARING

The main purpose of worksharing is to reduce the unemployment caused by an inadequate demand for labour in the economy. Although the overall demand for labour can increase if the government adopts an expansionary monetary and fiscal policy, governments are reluctant to stimulate the economy in this way because they fear increasing inflation. In the latter half of the 1970s the governments of Canada and Ontario were so concerned about inflation that they adopted restrictive policies and tolerated the resulting higher unemployment levels. Since governments have demonstrated that they are unwilling or unable to stimulate the economy sufficiently to employ the rapidly growing labour force and reduce unemployment, alternative ways of dealing with unemployment are urgently needed.

The single most important policy change that the government can make to facilitate worksharing is to permit employees who are worksharing to draw Unemployment Insurance benefits. The idea of such an arrangement is that since a larger number of workers will share the reduction in employment which otherwise would have been borne by the laid-off workers they should also share the unemployment benefits which the laid-off workers would have received. The objective of the government is to pay the same total UI benefits, but to achieve a more equitable distribution of the work reduction, the UI benefits, and the increased leisure time than would occur in a layoff.

In our view the objective of such a policy change is to eliminate the unintended bias toward layoffs which exists in the present legislation. We feel a new program should be neutral in this respect and thus as far as possible should parallel the provisions of the UI program available to laid-off workers. In particular, in order for a worksharing unit to be entitled to UI benefits the average employee in the unit would be subject to the normal regulations to qualify for benefits, the same waiting period would apply before benefits could be drawn, and there would be an identical maximum period of eligibility during which UI benefits could be received.

In 1977 the Unemployment Insurance Act was amended by Bill C-24 to permit a limited number of experimental worksharing projects along the lines suggested above to provide the basis for a more informed assessment of the worksharing option. The Canada Employment and Immigration Commission experimented with two basic models. The first model attempted to avoid the impact of a layoff arising from a temporary reduction in available employment. Twenty-three firms were in this category.[1] The second model attempts to cushion the impact of an anticipated permanent or long-term layoff. Only one firm was in this category.[2]

The design of the experimental program contained modifications. The normal two-week waiting period before UI benefits could be received was eliminated, the period of time for which the employees were entitled to draw worksharing UI benefits was not limited to the normal eligibility period, and, if layoffs occurred following the termination of the worksharing program, the laid-off employees would be entitled to their normal UI benefits in addition to any UI benefits received under the worksharing program. The purpose of these modifications appears to have been to encourage participation by groups which might normally be hesitant to take part in an experimental program. Such provisions would increase the cost of the pilot projects, but they very likely would not be included in a permanent economy-wide worksharing scheme.

Evaluations of the experimental projects are being conducted by consultants for the CEIC, but the results have not been made public. It is our understanding that there have been positive and negative results. On the positive side the programs have succeeded in avoiding potential layoffs. The reaction of the managers, employees, and local union leaders involved in the pilot programs has been overwhelmingly posi-

1 Some of the firms included in the first-model experiments were Atlantic Sleep Products of Scoudouc and Moncton, New Brunswick, and IKO Industries of Brampton and Hawkesbury, Ontario.
2 The firm examined in the second-model experiment was Brunswick Mining and Smelting Corporation in Bathurst, New Brunswick.

tive. On the negative side, the consultants have pointed out a substantially higher cost in terms of UI benefits paid out than would have occurred with layoffs and regular UI benefits. In fact most of the cost increases resulted from the experience of two firms which during the experiment had their period of eligibility extended. Most of these cost increases, however, appear to have been due to the special provisions of the worksharing experiments outlined above and likely would not be present in a permanent worksharing program.

If a permanent worksharing program is to be implemented two further important policy changes are needed in addition to the revision of the Unemployment Insurance Act to allow worksharing employees to draw benefits. First, the ceiling levels on income subject to UI contributions should be altered. These ceiling levels were originally fixed because the benefits drawn are proportionate to earnings and the government wanted to prevent employees whose incomes were substantially above the average from drawing unduly high benefits. But the ceiling levels on earnings subject to contributions have had the completely unintended side-effect of providing a bias against worksharing and in favour of layoffs, because, as noted above, worksharing tends to reduce the proportion of the firm's payroll that is above the ceiling and thus exempt from UI contributions.

Fortunately, it is easy to eliminate this bias while retaining the purpose of the ceilings: the solution is to place a ceiling on the average *hourly* earnings subject to contribution rather than on the average weekly or annual earnings. This change will eliminate the unintended and undesirable bias against worksharing that exists in the present laws without incurring any significant additional administrative costs. We recommend this policy change without reservation.

A further deterrent to the acceptance of worksharing by firms is the fact that when workers are laid off the firm saves the cost of any contributions to health insurance plans that it would have made on behalf of the laid-off workers had they remained on the job. The Canadian Labour Congress (1978, 29), among others, called for a government policy change that would require firms to continue paying fringe benefits for workers who are laid off. The costs and benefits of this proposal need to be assessed. Without making a recommendation, we simply note that such a policy would remove one of the disincentives to worksharing.

The implications of worksharing for the firm
An important advantage of worksharing to the firm is that fewer workers are lost to other firms during worksharing than during a layoff. Since firms will need to replace fewer workers, when normal production resumes they will save hiring and training costs. Savings of this kind will depend on the type of training needed, conditions in the labour market, and other factors, but a preliminary analysis indicates that they may in some cases outweigh any rise in costs due to increased employer contributions to fringe benefits. Worksharing may also increase productivity by reducing absenteeism and worker fatigue and by eliminating the necessity of reallocating jobs when workers are laid off.

The implications of worksharing for the worker
Clearly, worksharing is of greatest benefit to workers who would otherwise have been laid off. It enables them to avoid the reduction of income that accompanies unemployment and causes serious economic problems, particularly for heads of households, and it saves them from the loss of self-esteem often associated with unemployment. Research has shown that the stress resulting from unemployment significantly increases alcoholism, crime, mental illness, and suicides (Brenner 1976). Much of the loss of self-esteem and psychological stress associated with unemployment stems from the decline of income and status compared to one's peers. Because worksharing produces a more equitable distribution of the reduction of income a worksharing employee suffers no relative change in status among his fellow employees. Thus, worksharing eliminates the large component of stress that results from the change in relative positions of employees within a peer group. This important benefit of worksharing is not widely recognized.

Worksharing can also benefit those workers who would not have been laid off. In the hypothetical worksharing case considered in Chapter 2, this group comprises the 80 per cent of employees who agree to work four days a week instead of five to prevent a layoff of 20 per cent of their fellow employees. If the normal five-day, forty-hour work week reflects the amount that the typical employee wants to work at the prevailing wage, then in the absence of UI benefits it will obviously be a sacrifice to him to agree to work less than the full work week. A worker may be willing to make such a sacrifice out of a feeling of altruism for his fellows, particularly in unionized firms, where feelings of solidarity are highly developed. That such feelings of solidarity do exist among workers in Ontario is demonstrated by that fact that approximately 62,000 employees have negotiated worksharing provisions in their collective agreements even *without* supplementary UI benefits to offset the loss of income resulting from worksharing.

If UI benefits were made available to offset the loss of income due to worksharing the analysis would change considerably. Worksharing would then be much more attractive to the employees who would not have been laid off. Under current UI regulations, benefits amount to 60 per cent of weekly earnings up to the ceiling. In our hypothetical worksharing scheme workers who reduce their work week from five days to four would thus receive four days' regular pay plus 60 per cent of a day's pay for the one day a week on which they are 'unemployed.' Workers therefore lose only (0.4 times 20 per cent) 8 per cent in weekly earnings even though the number of hours they work has dropped by 20 per cent. In other words, an employee will receive 4.6 days' pay for four days' work. If the normal work-week is forty hours, UI-assisted worksharing will give the employee approximately thirty-seven hours' pay for thirty-two hours' work.

Because the income tax system is progressive, an 8 per cent reduction in gross pay will reduce take-home pay by slightly less than 8 per cent. Probably the easiest way to understand this is to consider that, if gross pay increased by 8 per cent, after-tax income would increase by less than 8 per cent, because the extra income would be taxed at a marginal tax rate higher than it was before the pay increase. Conversely, if gross pay decreased by 8 per cent, after-tax income would decrease by less than 8 per cent, because the marginal tax rate would be lower than it was before the decrease.

The exact amount of the reduction will depend on the employee's marginal and average tax rates, which in turn will depend on his gross income and the tax exemptions he is entitled to claim. To illustrate: if an employee with a marginal tax rate of 40 per cent and an average tax rate of 20 per cent received an 8 per cent reduction in gross pay, his take-home pay would decline by only 6 per cent.[3]

---

3 Denote after-tax income by X, before-tax income by Y, the average tax rate by atr and the marginal tax rate by mtr. The definition of the average tax rate, atr $\equiv (Y - X)/Y$, implies $X = (1 - \text{atr})Y$. The definition of the marginal

The use of UI benefits to offset the loss of income due to work-sharing reduces the price of leisure to the worker. Instead of having to give up one hour's pay to reduce the work week by one hour, the 60 per cent UI benefits allows the worker to give up only 40 per cent of an hour's pay to gain the same one-hour reduction. If the typical worker were employed for his preferred number of hours each week before worksharing, the reduction in the price of leisure would cause the worker to want to consume more leisure, i.e. to work fewer hours.

This analysis leads to a very important conclusion. If the typical worker is employed for his preferred number of hours before work-sharing, the introduction of UI benefits to offset the income lost during worksharing will cause even employees who would *not* have been subject to layoff to prefer to engage in some worksharing in their own self-interest. This conclusion applies both to workers with a permanent attachment to the labour force and to those with a temporary attachment.

This conclusion can easily be demonstrated in formal economic terms with the indifference curve analysis from Chapter 3. A worker is initially in equilibrium at point A in Figure 13, that is, he is working forty hours a week, and the marginal rate of substitution of income for leisure equals the wage rate. The introduction of UI benefits for income lost through worksharing makes the budget line 'flatter' to the right of point A. The new equilibrium for the worker is point B, at which there

---

tax rate, mtr $\equiv d\,(Y - X)/dY$, implies $dX = (1 - \text{mtr})dY$. These two expressions together imply that the proportional change in after-tax income, dX/X, is related to the proportional change in before-tax income, dY/Y, by the following formula:

$$\frac{dX}{X} = \frac{(1 - \text{mtr})}{(1 - \text{atr})}\frac{dY}{Y}$$

In the worksharing example mtr is 0.4, atr is 0.2, and dY/Y is 8 per cent, implying that dX/X is 6 per cent. A specific numerical example may also be useful. If weekly earnings initially are \$200/wk and atr = 0.2, the initial after-tax income is $(1 - 0.2)$ \$200, or \$160/wk. An 8 per cent reduction in earnings implies a reduction of 0.08 (\$200), or \$16/wk. With an mtr of 0.4, this implies a reduction in after-tax income of only $(1 - 0.4)$ \$16, or \$9.60 per wk. The percentage reduction in after-tax income is this \$9.60/\$160 = 0.06, or 6 per cent.

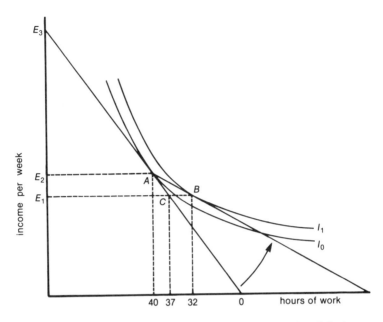

Figure 13   The effect of UI benefits on worker attitudes toward worksharing

This figure shows how even workers who are not likely to be laid off can prefer UI-supported worksharing to working full-time. The worker in question is initially in equilibrium at point A on indifference curve I_0. The introduction of UI-supported worksharing shifts the worker's budget line upward — i.e. it makes it 'flatter' — to the right of point A. In effect, leisure time has become 'cheaper' and the worker is able to 'buy' extra hours of leisure at the 'cost' of less of his earnings than he would have had to forgo without UI support. The worker's new equilibrium is at point B on indifference curve I_1; though he earns less income than he would have earned at equilibrium point A, he is working far fewer hours and obtaining a higher level of satisfaction in doing so. In fact, though he is earning the same income under the worksharing arrangement as he would have earned in 37 hours' work without the worksharing arrangement, he is working only 32 hours for it.

is a decrease in the number of hours worked each week. The worker achieves a higher level of satisfaction by engaging in some worksharing.

Although this analysis indicates that a typical employee will want to undertake worksharing under some circumstances, it certainly does not mean that he will welcome all worksharing proposals. If a particular scheme imposes more worksharing (i.e. a greater reduction in hours)

than an individual wants, it may make him worse off than he would be
if there were no worksharing. Furthermore, some employees may be
overemployed or underemployed in a standard work week, as we noted
in Chapter 3. The overemployed will be even more attracted to worksharing and the underemployed less attracted to worksharing than the
employee who is satisfied with the standard work week.

The implications of worksharing for unions
The mixture of responses that unions have made to worksharing is
consistent with the variety of advantages and disadvantages of this
scheme to unions set forth in Chapter 3. Some unions have made strong
and highly publicized statements against worksharing; for example, the
United Steelworkers of America in 1977 emphatically rejected Prime
Minister Trudeau's suggestion that worksharing be implemented to
avoid layoffs at Inco in Sudbury. And the Canadian Labour Congress
stated flatly in its brief to the Commission of Inquiry into Redundancies and Layoffs that 'the Congress is opposed to worksharing
schemes' (1978, 36).

But there is less-well-known evidence indicating union support for
worksharing. First, the Steelworkers themselves participated in one of
the pilot worksharing projects at Brunswick Mining and Smelting in
New Brunswick. Second, some unions have negotiated worksharing provisions even without the incentive of a UI subsidy for the income lost
through worksharing. Third, the Canadian Labour Congress has repeat-
edly called for restrictions on overtime and a reduction in the standard
work-week from forty hours to thirty-two hours (1978, 29); although
this proposal is often accompanied by a demand for forty hours' pay
for thirty-two hours' work, our analysis of UI-assisted worksharing
indicates that its net effect on employee income and hours would be
fairly close to this demand. Finally, outside Canada, the New York State
AFL-CIO in 1975 supported an attempt to amend New York State laws
to allow UI benefits for worksharing (Levitan and Belous 1977a, 18).

We conclude that there are differences of opinion within the union
movement regarding the merits of worksharing, and the topic is still
open to debate. We are confident that the union movement's support or
lack of support for worksharing will ultimately rest on a careful consideration of its potential costs and benefits to Canadian workers.

The advantages of worksharing to the government and society
The most obvious advantage of worksharing to the government is that its widespread adoption will reduce the measured unemployment rate. It is important, however, to consider whether this is a real benefit to society or just a way of disguising unemployment.

It is true that, generally speaking, worksharing does not change the total number of hours of employment in the economy; nor does it affect the total amount of wages, UI benefits, and leisure time that workers enjoy.[3] But worksharing does alter the *distribution* of these factors, and the distribution is crucial.

In our view the use of layoffs instead of worksharing is both inequitable and inefficient. Layoffs are inequitable because they shift the full burden of a reduction in employment caused by a decline in aggregate demand to a small fraction of the labour force. It is unfair that a relatively small group of individuals who are not responsible for reductions in aggregate demand should bear the consequences of those reductions, especially when the reductions are induced or tolerated by governments to lower inflation, a goal that benefits society as a whole.

Layoffs are inefficient because they produce a distribution of wages and leisure in society that is not Pareto-optimal.[4] Consider a layoff in which a small fraction of the work force is unemployed and receiving UI benefits and the rest of the labour force is employed full-time. If the unemployed and employed are permitted to engage in 'trade,' that is, if unemployed workers are allowed to exchange some of their leisure hours (and UI benefits) for some hours of employment (and wage income), both groups may benefit. The indifference curve analysis above suggests that this is true. Layoffs distribute leisure time and employment inefficiently, so that some persons have 'too much' leisure and others have 'too much' employment. Worksharing helps solve this problem.

One of the most serious and compelling arguments against worksharing is that the reduction in measured unemployment it achieves

---

3 One qualification is that total UI benefits will increase to the extent that the government is unable to prevent firms who would not have laid off workers from fraudulently obtaining worksharing benefits.
4 That is, layoffs produce a distribution in which it is still possible to make some workers better off without simultaneously making others worse off.

may divert governments from the more important goals of increasing aggregate demand and decreasing the unemployment that results from a deficiency of demand; and there is no doubt that full employment is preferable to either worksharing or layoffs. But governments must fight inflation as well as unemployment, and given the unfavourable (short-run) tradeoff between inflation and unemployment the Canadian economy will probably experience periods of high unemployment in the future. In these circumstances the real policy choice is not between worksharing and full employment but between worksharing and layoffs.

In assessing the cost of a worksharing program to the government it is necessary to remember that employees at firms which would have reduced the number of hours worked each week without the program would also be eligible for worksharing benefits. Hammermesh (1979) calls this the 'windfall effect' of a worksharing program. The data indicate, however, that this problem is of little practical importance in Canada. In May 1979, for example, only 0.7 per cent of Canadian employees were on 'short-time' (*Labour Force*, May 1979). Many of these short-time workers would not be eligible for worksharing benefits if the program specified a minimum reduction in hours for eligibility. (For example, the Canadian experimental program specified a minimum 20 per cent reduction in hours.)

Hammermesh also points out that a substantial portion of worksharing benefits can accrue to employees in industries such as construction, where there is a regular seasonal variation in the number of hours worked each week. He suggests that if the government wants to make firms with seasonal fluctuations in hours ineligible for worksharing benefits it can include a 'trigger' so that the worksharing plan will be implemented only when the aggregate unemployment rate exceeds a specified level.

Hammermesh further proposes the use of an experience-rating of firms to prevent abuses in applying worksharing benefits. An experience-rating is a system relating a firm's Unemployment Insurance contributions to its record of layoffs. Since experience-rating is not used in Canada, we suggest that it be introduced.

Another problem with UI-subsidized worksharing is the possibility that firms reducing weekly hours as a result of supply preferences on the part of their workers may attempt to claim worksharing benefits.

The agency administering a worksharing program will need to distinguish such cases from those of firms using worksharing legitimately in response to a fall in demand. The main criterion should be whether or not the decrease in weekly hours per worker is accompanied by an increase in the number of workers employed; if it is, then the cause of worksharing is probably not a reduction in the demand for labour, and the firm will be ineligible for worksharing UI benefits. A complication may arise, however, if the firm waits until demand falls to implement a shorter work week that is really intended to satisfy worker preferences. This problem will not be easy to solve, but it is unlikely to be very important because the changes in the number of hours that employees want to work each week are usually small and evolve over long periods of time.

Finally, it is worthwhile to consider how large a reduction in the unemployment rate worksharing can actually achieve. Worksharing has the potential to help only those who lose their jobs through a temporary layoff; it does not help the unemployed who have left their jobs voluntarily or those who are new entrants or re-entrants to the labour force. Canadian data indicate that in December 1978, when the unemployment rate was 8.1 per cent, about half of the unemployed had lost their jobs involuntarily (*Labour Force*, December 1978). It is not clear how many of these job losses are temporary and how many are permanent, but a conservative estimate of the proportion of persons on temporary layoff who are potential targets for worksharing is 1.5 to 2.0 per cent of the labour force.

In Germany, which has a well-developed worksharing scheme, the number of persons who are worksharing is roughly equal to the number of persons who are unemployed (Henle 1976, 8). If this relationship holds for Canada, about 8 per cent of the labour force will be worksharing. The hypothetical worksharing scheme used in our model assumed that one-fifth of those involved would have been unemployed without worksharing. If this proportion is used, it implies that if 8 per cent of the labour force were worksharing then the unemployment rate would be reduced by one-fifth of 8 per cent, or 1.6 per cent.

At this point we caution the reader that worksharing should not be regarded as a panacea for Canada's economic problems. It can reduce unemployment, but since it applies only to workers on temporary layoff the potential reduction in the unemployment rate is probably about 1 or 2 per cent. Furthermore, unless the ceilings on contributions to UI, CPP, and Workmen's Compensation are specified in hourly rather than weekly terms, worksharing may increase the cost of employer contributions to those plans. Finally, there appears to be substantial disagreement within the union movement regarding the benefits of worksharing. Despite these qualifications, however, our view is that a UI-assisted worksharing program can be a useful complement to macroeconomic policy.

THE POLICY IMPLICATIONS OF THE MODEL FOR JOBSHARING

Conditions under which firms will support jobsharing
Chapter 2 showed that a firm that is jobsharing will incur higher labour costs than one employing full-time workers, because the costs of fringe benefits, hiring, training, and supervision are all greater. For this reason, if wage rates are equal, employers will prefer full-time employees to jobsharing employees. There are three circumstances, however, under which jobsharing is likely to become attractive to employers: when there is a shortage of full-time workers at given relative wages and an excess supply of workers who want to jobshare; when a wage differential between full-time employees and jobsharing employees develops that is sufficient to offset the increased costs; and when employer contributions for fringe benefits that are pure quasi-fixed costs are prorated and employees wishing to jobshare agree to pay the rest of the cost themselves.

The advantages of jobsharing to the worker
Employees will desire to jobshare under a number of conditions. We observed in Chapters 3 and 4 that women are among the persons most receptive to employment-sharing, and our demographic projections indicate that the proportion of women in the labour force will increase.

In addition an important trend in the labour force has been the increase in the number of multiple-earner families. In such families the earnings of one family member increase the non-wage incomes of the other family members. As demonstrated in Chapter 3, an increase in non-wage income generally reduces the number of hours that an individual wishes to work each week. Thus, an increase in multiple-earner families is likely to produce an increased interest in jobsharing.

Although the demographic projections above show some decrease in the proportion of older men in the labour force, the numbers may be increased if the recent raising of the mandatory retirement age in the United States from 65 to 70 inspires a similar development in Canada. Older workers are very receptive to employment-sharing and may want to extend their careers by working less than full time.

Furthermore, older workers who have remained in the labour force tend to be those who are more professional and highly skilled. Perhaps older skilled workers will consent in future to share jobs with unskilled young persons, so that the participation rate of older workers would tend to increase. Jobs of this kind may be more attractive than those usually available to young persons on a part-time basis since they will make it possible to acquire a skill on the job. Such jobsharing may reduce turnover and absenteeism among young people.

Jobsharing and government policy
What can the government do to encourage jobsharing? First, as we have previously recommended, it can remove the current bias in the economy against jobsharing by specifying the ceilings on contributions to UI, CPP, and Workmen's Compensation in terms of hourly rather than annual earnings. Second, it can use training and unemployment insurance funds to share the costs of this type of jobsharing with firms that may be deterred by the extra costs. This arrangement will increase on-the-job skill training and enable older workers to extend their careers. The likelihood that the costs of pensions and other old-age assistance will increase rapidly in future provides a further reason for giving older workers the opportunity to maintain their attachment to the labour force through jobsharing.

POLICY IMPLICATIONS OF THE MODEL FOR
PART-TIME EMPLOYMENT

Part-time work is the most widespread of the three types of employment-sharing discussed in this volume. This section examines the likely future developments in part-time employment and the role of government policy in these developments.

Demographic trends favouring part-time employment
The demographic trends outlined earlier imply that the potential supply of persons willing to work part-time will increase in the coming years. Though there will be fewer young workers in the labour force the number of prime-age females will grow. This change in the age distribution of the potential supply of part-time labour suggests that part-time jobs usually taken by young people – particularly such jobs as distributing newspapers, summer camp employment, and carnival and exhibition work – may become more difficult to fill. It has generally been the case, as our data on unemployment showed, that the unemployment rate for youth (under age 25) seeking part-time employment is less than that for youth seeking full-time employment. The shortage of available labour may in turn lead to increases in the relative wages in jobs that have traditionally been among the lowest-paid in the labour market.

Most part-time employment has been accepted voluntarily by persons with other responsibilities such as going to school or maintaining a household. Furthermore, the decline in the birth rate suggests that fewer couples are choosing to have children. These couples may desire to reduce the number of hours they work each week in order to consume more leisure with their combined incomes.

Some problems with part-time employment
Certain problems must be solved if part-time work is to win more widespread acceptance. First, the conflict between employers and trade unions over the hiring of part-time workers must be settled. Employers may want to hire part-time workers to meet recurring peak loads or sudden temporary increases in demand. But unions often oppose the hiring of part-time workers because it may deprive full-time workers of opportunities to earn overtime pay and, if part-time workers are not included in the bargaining unit, it may reduce the strength of the union in the labour force. Even if part-time workers are included in the bargaining unit their commitment to the goals of the union may be suspect, and they may be thought to be concerned only with their own

short-term interests. The government must determine the place that part-time employees will occupy in collective bargaining units, especially if there is a trend toward introducing the type of jobsharing discussed above.

Second, the structural barriers to part-time employment must be removed. A structural barrier occurs when employers are unwilling or unable to convert unfilled full-time jobs into part-time jobs for which a labour supply is available. Structural barriers to part-time employment can be both psychological and legislative: psychological when a firm is not prepared to consider the economic feasibility of using part-time workers to fill vacancies, and legislative when governments fix the financial contributions that employers must make on behalf of their employees in such a way as to favour the hiring of a smaller number of full-time workers rather than a larger number of part-time workers (see Chapter 2).

The developments discussed above show that the increase in the proportion of the labour force working part-time is likely to persist. Though it is possible that if a very high proportion of the labour force wanted to work part-time productivity would ultimately decrease, now and in the foreseeable future part-time employment seems to be a very positive development. Persons engaged in part-time employment and those who might be brought into part-time work can be viewed as a long-term resource able to meet the needs that can arise from a general excess of demand. The hiring of older workers part-time to train younger part-time workers can provide benefits to both society and the individuals involved.

SUGGESTIONS FOR FURTHER RESEARCH

The following research topics are suggested to explore both the experience of employment-sharing and the potential for encouraging it.
— A study of the extent to which persons now working full-time actually prefer part-time work. To find out how many persons are involuntarily overemployed a special question can be added to the labour force survey periodically.
— Improving the data on part-time employment. The questions asked in the labour force survey about the reasons for not wanting full-time

work are somewhat vague. For example, it is possible to confuse 'going to school' with the general category 'do not want full-time work.' This confusion can be avoided by adopting the distinction between voluntary and involuntary part-time work that is used in the United States survey.

– A detailed examination of the wages of persons engaged in part-time work. In order to find out in what kinds of jobs persons are working part-time, and hence to gain some idea of the potential for employment-sharing, a detailed examination can be made of census data for each occupation and industry for 1961 and 1971 and eventually for 1981. The labour force survey material discussed in Chapter 4 deals only with broad groupings and provides no data on earnings. This shortcoming can be remedied by using census data.

– An analysis of the information available on cases of worksharing in the light of the theoretical framework developed in this study. As we noted earlier, several worksharing projects have been undertaken in Canada during the last few years. We suggest that these projects be examined using the factors identified in Chapters 2 and 3 to predict the possibility of success or failure in such programs. For example, our analysis shows that firms employing mainly prime-age males will be unlikely to engage in worksharing unless large and protracted layoffs are expected and unless the income lost through worksharing will be less than or equal to that lost through a prolonged layoff. Using these factors a complete analysis of recent experiments in worksharing which have been conducted by the Canada Employment and Immigration Commission (see above) should enable us to find out if we have identified the factors most likely to predict whether a worksharing program will be introduced.

– An analysis of the possibilities of jobsharing in various industries and occupations. Case studies of possible jobsharing might be conducted in one or more of the following situations: (i) a high proportion of women or older workers or both, (ii) an inability to recruit full-time workers because of the lack of qualified persons, (iii) a likelihood that an adequate supply of persons for part-time work or jobsharing would be available, especially if (iv) the jobs require skills that could be learned while jobsharing.

6
Summary and conclusions

This final chapter summarizes the findings of our examination of work-sharing, jobsharing, and part-time employment. We first discuss the three types of costs with which firms are confronted, fixed, variable, and quasi-fixed. We then present the results of a computer simulation analysis used to evaluate the effects of hypothetical worksharing and jobsharing plans on a firm's contributions to Unemployment Insurance, Canada Pension Plan, and Workmen's Compensation. Next we discuss the attitudes of workers and trade unions toward employment-sharing and the factors that guide them. These supply and demand perspectives are then brought together through the results of some tests that were applied to statistics on the present extent of employment-sharing. The last section summarizes the policy implications of our research.

FIXED, VARIABLE, AND QUASI-FIXED COSTS

In Chapter 2 we identified three kinds of costs: fixed, variable, and quasi-fixed costs. Fixed and variable costs are unaffected by employment-sharing, but quasi-fixed costs, i.e. those costs related to the number of *employees* rather than the total number of *hours* they are employed, are important in analysing the effects of employment-sharing. Since employment-sharing spreads a given total number of hours of labour among a greater number of employees than would be required if all worked a full week, the effect of employment-sharing on a firm's cost is directly related to the size of the firm's quasi-fixed costs. Some fringe benefits have elements of both quasi-fixed costs and variable costs. Benefits such as Unemployment Insurance, the Canada Pension Plan, and Workmen's Compensation require the payment of a fixed percentage of an employee's annual income but set a ceiling on the total earnings per employee subject to contribution. At wage levels below the ceiling these benefits are pure variable costs; employment-sharing at such wage levels does not increase costs and may even decrease them if there is a minimum on earnings subject to contribution. At wage levels above the ceiling these benefits become pure quasi-fixed costs; employment-sharing under these circumstances increases costs to the employer.

THE EFFECT OF WORKSHARING ON COSTS

In the worksharing plan analysed in Chapter 2 a layoff of twenty per cent of the employees is avoided by retaining five employees who work a four-day week instead of keeping only four employees full-time for five days and laying one employee off. The resulting increase in employer contribution costs for the fringe benefits named above depends on the level of annual employee earnings. For employees earning $20,000 a year in 1978, worksharing increases the firm's annual contribution costs by $231.75 a year for each full-time employee, an increase that corresponds to 1.15 per cent of total labour costs. But when employees earn only $8000 a year worksharing has virtually no effect on the firm's contribution costs (if it is assumed that the firm does not pay health insurance premiums for employees at this level of earnings).

Worksharing has other effects on a firm's labour costs which may be even more important than the firm's contributions to various fringe benefits but which are more difficult to estimate empirically. One of these is the reduction of hiring and training costs. Employees who are worksharing are less likely to take a job elsewhere than those who are laid off; as a result, it will be necessary to replace fewer workers when demand increases and the firm resumes its normal work schedule. Precise estimates of the potential savings could not be made with the data available to us. However, our rough estimates indicate that the use

of worksharing rather than layoffs can save a firm about 1.7 per cent of
its gross payroll. Since the size of this saving outweighs the costs of
increased fringe benefit contributions (estimated above to be 1.15 per
cent at most) worksharing may actually save the firm money. Clearly,
further research is needed to obtain more precise estimates.

Worksharing has four other effects on labour costs that we mention
but do not attempt to estimate empirically. First, worksharing may
reduce absenteeism by allowing employees more time during the week
to recover from illnesses, conduct essential personal business, or engage
in leisure-time activities. Second, productivity may either increase because employee fatigue has declined or decrease because the 'start-up
time' at the beginning of the week is longer. Third, worksharing may
delay productivity increases which would have resulted from a firm not
hiring back as many persons as it laid off. In this situation the layoff
period is used as an opportunity to assess the number of employees
who are needed to meet production requirements. In the absence of
layoffs, however, these productivity changes would become apparent
over a longer period of time. Finally, worksharing may reduce labour
costs by eliminating the administrative costs of the 'bumping' process
often associated with layoffs and by preventing a rise in average costs
due to the layoff of lower-paid junior workers.

THE EFFECT OF JOBSHARING ON COSTS

In the representative jobsharing plan analysed in Chapter 2, one
full-time employee is replaced by two half-time employees. It is
assumed that, where possible, the employer's contribution to fringe
benefits are prorated, so that costs will not be affected by jobsharing.
For statutory programs such as UI, CPP, and Workmen's Compensation,
however, prorating is not possible, and the effect on costs was analysed.
The results indicate that jobsharing has no significant effect when full-
time employees earn $8000 a year or less, but when they earn $20,000
a year it increases the firm's contribution costs by 1.91 per cent.

Jobsharing is also likely to increase hiring and training costs, in
contrast to worksharing, which reduces these costs. The reason is
simply that jobsharing doubles the number of employees, so that if
turnover is not affected twice as many employees will have to be hired

and trained during any time period. On the other hand it is very likely that jobsharing will reduce turnover, so that hiring and training costs will not be doubled. Unless turnover rates are cut in half, however, a net increase in hiring and training costs will still result.

Jobsharing is likely to increase administrative costs because more employees must be supervised and there is a greater need to communicate work instructions. On the positive side, jobsharing may reduce turnover, as indicated above. It also has the potential to increase productivity either by lowering absenteeism or by reducing worker fatigue.

A further cost advantage of jobsharing is flexibility; workers sharing a job could fill in for each other during absences, holidays, and periods of hiring and training.

There may be some analogies between the current discussion of jobsharing and that which took place a decade ago on the subject of flexible working hours. It is now generally accepted that flexible working hours (FWH) has proved to be cost effective by reducing 'absenteeism, overtime, staff turnover and non-productive time, as well as [producing] increased productivity and enhanced morale and labour relations' (FitzGibbon 1980). At first there was considerable reservation about FWH and only some tentative experiments. Now FWH is accepted in sectors that do not involve production processes, such as insurance and provincial governments and the clerical staff of manufacturing and distributing companies. It may well be that in the next decade jobsharing will also become an accepted part of certain sectors of the economy where its unique features can benefit both employees and employers.

THE WORKERS' ATTITUDES TOWARD WORKSHARING

The number of hours a week that a person desires to work will be influenced by factors such as the type of job available, the wage rate, the amount of income from other sources, and the individual's family and personal responsibilities.

This study is concerned with workers' attitudes toward a worksharing scheme in which the workers receive unemployment insurance for their 'short-time' – in our example the fifth day when the work week is reduced from five days to four days by worksharing.

For workers who would otherwise be laid off the benefits of worksharing are fairly clear. In addition to maintaining approximately 92 per cent of their normal weekly income, they maintain their work skills, their social group, and the self-esteem that derives from employment in our society.

What is less obvious is that even those workers who would not have been laid off will generally prefer some amount of worksharing when it is accompanied by the UI subsidy. The reason is that the worksharing scheme allows the worker to attain an extra day of leisure with a much smaller reduction in income than would normally be the case.

Worksharing will be preferred even more strongly by those workers who are overemployed in their current jobs, i.e. workers who would prefer to work less than the standard forty-hour week but are unable to do so because of a lack of suitable part-time jobs in their industry or occupation. From theoretical considerations one would expect the overemployed group to contain a high proportion of young workers without dependents, female workers who typically carry the bulk of the workload in the home, and older workers, some of whom may wish less demanding schedules. The empirical tests of our model explaining the incidence of worksharing provisions among industries gave results consistent with these tendencies.

In actual experiments with UI-assisted worksharing in unionized firms the reaction of the employees and the union leaders at the local level was overwhelmingly favourable. However, the Canadian Labour Congress has strongly opposed worksharing, apparently from concern that the use of worksharing rather than layoffs by seniority would result in the seniority principle being bypassed in other areas and concern that the use of worksharing might divert the government from attempting to achieve full employment.

THE WORKERS' ATTITUDES TOWARDS JOBSHARING

As with worksharing, our economic analysis predicts that jobsharing will be most heavily favoured by persons who are overemployed at their current jobs – young persons, married women, and older workers. Although no systematic statistics on jobsharing are available, this prediction is in our view supported by experience. The numerous jobsharing experiments of which we are aware involve almost exclusively married women in occupations such as librarian, teacher, and nurse. Our empirical analysis of part-time work also confirms these demographic factors in preferences towards employment-sharing.

Trade union attitudes toward jobsharing are difficult to predict, since each union is a unique combination of persons and has interests of its own as an institution. Unions will tend to support jobsharing if such a plan gives their members more flexibility and opportunities for employment and if it boosts union membership by increasing the number of skilled workers. They will tend to oppose jobsharing if they view it as a way of keeping wages down and reducing union solidarity or bargaining power, or if it reduces the income they receive through membership dues.

TESTING THE MODEL

In Chapter 4 we brought supply and demand together by testing an economic model of employment-sharing. Two tests of the worksharing model were made. In the first, data from collective agreements in Ontario that included worksharing provisions were compared in a qualitative way with an estimate of the likelihood that a worksharing agreement would occur in any given industry. These estimates were made using combined measures from the demand and supply sides: on the demand side average weekly earnings of wage earners were used as an indication of quasi-fixed costs; on the supply side the percentage of female employees, the percentage of part-time employees, and the percentage of employees in the prime-age group were used to indicate the probability that workers will agree to workshare. The model predicted the actual incidence of worksharing correctly in nine out of eleven cases. In the second test the collective agreements data were analysed using multiple regression analysis. Our model was able to explain about half of the total variation in the incidence of worksharing provisions among industries. Generally, the results were statistically significant and in accord with the predictions from the economic model.

The employment-sharing model was further tested by examining the available Canadian and U.S. data on various aspects of part-time employment to determine whether they corroborate our theory. The trends in these data conform to the expectations raised in the theory discussed in Chapter 3. The lowest incidence of part-time work occurs among prime-age male workers, who most closely resemble the category of persons with a permanent attachment to the labour force; the highest incidence of part-time employment is found among young workers, both male and female, who might be characterized as having a temporary attachment to the labour force; and the next highest incidence is found among older workers. The lowest incidence of part-time employment among women is found in the prime-age group, but it is still far above that among prime-age males – more than ten times as high. This finding suggests that there is a substantial component of prime-age women who have a temporary attachment to the labour force.

The major reasons that those working part-time cited for doing so was that they were not seeking full-time work or were going to school. Part-time jobs tended to be in low-wage sales and service occupations. Although young people have an unemployment rate almost twice the overall unemployment rate, the rate for young workers seeking part-time work was lower than that for young workers seeking full-time work. In total, however, part-time workers have a higher unemployment rate than full-time workers because of the high unemployment rate among male part-time workers.

THE POLICY IMPLICATIONS OF THE MODEL

From the analysis in this study we have drawn several implications for public policy. First, the current practice of specifying the ceiling level for a firm's contributions to Unemployment Insurance, the Canada Pension Plan, and Workmen's Compensation as a percentage of an employee's annual earnings creates a completely unintended bias against worksharing and in favour of layoffs. It also creates a bias against jobsharing and in favour of full-time employment. These biases can be eliminated while retaining the function of the ceilings by specifying the ceilings as a percentage of hourly rather than of annual earnings. We recommend this change in policy.

Second, though we think that the government must commit itself to a full-employment policy, if reductions in the demand for labour cannot be prevented, worksharing is a more equitable and efficient response than layoffs. To encourage worksharing rather than layoffs we recommend that the Unemployment Insurance Act be modified to permit employees who are worksharing to draw UI benefits to compensate partially for the reduction in their incomes. The government should therefore adopt permanently, after the experiments have been evaluated and appropriate revisions made, the modifications to the Act that were introduced on a limited provisional basis in August 1977 to allow worksharing employees to draw partial benefits.

We think UI-assisted worksharing is desirable because it is more equitable to share work than to allow a small fraction of the labour force to bear the burden of the unemployment that results from a reduction in aggregate demand while the great majority reap the benefits (reduced inflation). We think it is more efficient than layoffs because the savings to the firm in lower hiring and training costs are likely to more than offset any increases due to the greater costs of fringe benefits. Furthermore, worksharing results in a distribution of work, income, UI benefits, and leisure time that is more efficient[1] than the distribution resulting from layoffs.

Worksharing should not be regarded as a panacea for Canada's economic problems, however. It can reduce unemployment due to temporary layoffs, but it cannot affect unemployment among new entrants or re-entrants to the labour force or layoffs due to permanent plant closures. Our rough estimates suggest that a well-developed worksharing program can reduce the unemployment rate by between 1 and 2 per cent of the labour force.

Demographic trends suggest that changes in the composition of the labour force are likely to cause a decline in the number of young workers and a substantial increase in the number of married women in the labour force. These trends can, on balance, be expected to increase the number of people interested in jobsharing and part-time work.

The recommendation which we made above to change the ceilings on statutory fringe benefits from annual to hourly rates would also encourage jobsharing by increasing the costs saving.

---

1 It is more 'efficient' in the economic sense that some people can be made better off without anyone else having to be made worse off.

Another issue to be addressed is the status of part-time workers in bargaining units and collective agreements. In the past they have been caught in the conflict between management and the trade unions. Governments should ensure that the policies of the various labour relations boards do not specify bargaining units that inadvertently hinder the implementation of jobsharing.

Our impression, and it must remain only an impression because we have no hard data, is that there exist a substantial number of persons already in, or potentially in, the labour force who desire to share a job but lack opportunities. The main barrier to jobsharing appears to be concern by employers that costs will be increased. On the basis of the available evidence (e.g. Meier 1979) we are convinced that jobsharing can be cost-efficient especially when full-time labour is not available. The problem may be a lack of appreciation by employers of the cost reducing potential of jobsharing outlined above. To the extent this is true, government ought to encourage demonstration projects in appropriate industries and publish the results.

Finally, an employer will be more likely to experiment with jobsharing in a situation of full employment when it is difficult to obtain qualified labour for full-time jobs but when there are persons willing to work part-time. Therefore, by vigorously pursuing a full-employment policy the government will also be helping provide a welcome opportunity for jobsharing to develop in the economy.

References

BOLLMAN, RAYMOND D. (1978) 'Off-farm work by farmers: a study with a kinked demand for labour curve.' PHD thesis, University of Toronto

BRENNER, HARVEY (1976) *Estimating the Social Costs of National Economic Policy: Implications for Mental and Physical Health, and Criminal Aggression.* A study prepared for the Joint Economic Committee of the U.S. Congress (Washington: U.S. Government Printing Office)

CANADIAN LABOUR CONGRESS (1978) 'Submission to the inquiry into redundancies and layoffs.' Mimeo. (Ottawa)

CLARK, ROBERT (1977) *Adjusting Hours to Increase Jobs: An Analysis of the Options* (Washington: Congressional Research Service, Library of Congress)

DEUTERMANN, WILLIAM V. and SCOTT CAMPBELL BROWN (1978) 'Voluntary part-time workers: a growing part of the labor force.' *Monthly Labor Review*, 101, No. 6, 3-10

ECONOMIC COUNCIL OF CANADA (1976) *People and Jobs* (Ottawa)

FITZGIBBON, GEOFF (1980) 'Flexible working hours, the Canadian experience.' *Canadian Personnel and Industrial Relations Journal*, January 1980

HAMMERMESH, DANIEL S. (1979) 'Unemployment insurance, short-time compensation and the workweek.' In National Commission on Employment Policy, *Sharing Work to Combat Joblessness* (Washington, D.C.)

HENLE, PETER (1976) *Worksharing as an Alternative to Layoffs* (Washington: Congressional Research Service, Library of Congress)

LEVITAN, SAR A. and RICHARD S. BELOUS (1977a) 'Worksharing initiatives at home and abroad.' *Monthly Labor Review*, 100, No. 9, 16-20

— (1977b) *Shorter Hours, Shorter Weeks: Spreading the Work to Reduce Unemployment* (Baltimore: Johns Hopkins University Press)

MEIER, G.S. (1979) *A New Pattern for Quality of Work and Life* (Kalamazoo, Mich.: Upjohn Institute)

OI, WALTER (1962) 'Labor as a quasi-fixed factor.' *Journal of Political Economy*, 70, 538-55

OSTRY, SYLVIA and MAHMOOD ZAIDI (1979) *Labour Economics in Canada*, 3rd ed. (Toronto: Macmillan)

OWEN, JOHN D. (1978) 'Why part-time workers tend to be in low-wage jobs.' *Monthly Labor Review*, 101, No. 6, 11-14

REES, ALBERT (1973) *The Economics of Work and Pay* (New York: Harper and Row)

REID, FRANK (1980) 'Unemployment and inflation: an assessment of Canadian macroeconomic policy.' *Canadian Public Policy*, 6, 283-99

REID, FRANK and NOAH M. MELTZ (1979) 'Causes of shifts in the unemployment-vacancy relationship: an empirical analysis for Canada.' *Review of Economics and Statistics*, 61, 470-5

ROBERTSON, GORDON (1976) *Part-time Work in Ontario: 1966 to 1976*. (Toronto: Research Branch, Ontario Ministry of Labour, Employment Information Series, Number 20)

ROBERTSON, GORDON and JANE HUMPHREYS (1979) *Labour Turnover and Absenteeism in Selected Industries: Northwestern Ontario and Ontario*. Component Study Number 10, Northwestern Ontario Manpower Adjustment Study (Toronto: Ontario Ministry of Labour)

SADLIER-BROWN, PETER (1978) *Work Sharing in Canada: Problems and Possibilities* (Montreal: C.D. Howe Research Institute)

WEEKS, WENDY (1978) 'Collective bargaining and part-time work in Ontario.' *Industrial Relations/Relations Industrielles*, 33, 80-92